Fatimah Salleh and Margaret Olsen Hemming have given us a beautifully written commentary on hundreds of verses in the first third of the Book of Mormon. Although they avowedly write from the perspective of contemporary social justice advocates, their perspective is broader than that. They see in the Book of Mormon a picture of life as a hard journey—harsh, discouraging, contradictory—but one where God is always present to succor suffering travelers.

—Richard Bushman
author of *Joseph Smith: Rough Stone Rolling*

Across our differences—black, white, brown, indigenous, bond, free, male, female, gay, straight, living the principle, attending and tithing, or seeking another way altogether—what bonds LDS/Mormon people together is our relationship to the Book of Mormon. We have held it on our laps in cold early morning classrooms, stuffed it into our backpacks, purses, and suitcases, peered into our small bright screens searching out its verses, rested it on our nightstands, wept over it at our kitchen tables, argued over it on the internet, and wrestled with what it should mean to us individually and collectively. In this powerful new contribution to LDS scriptural study, Dr. Fatimah S. Salleh and Margaret Olsen Hemming have wrestled with the Book of Mormon in a whole new way: as a text that addresses inequality, trauma, dysfunction, and catastrophe and offers insights essential to achieving that dimension of Zion we call social justice. An essential companion for 21st century LDS/Mormon life. This book lifts my heart.

—Joanna Brooks
co-editor of *Mormon Feminism: Essential Writings*
and author of *Book of Mormon Girl*

The Book of Mormon For the Least of These will change the way you read the Book of Mormon, providing a profound and more reflective view of the events, teachings, and characters in the book than is traditional, and also offering a perspective on the book's principles of social justice that is missing in most Book of Mormon commentaries. A must read for those who take seriously their study of the Book of Mormon.

—Ignacio Garcia
professor of Western American History at
Brigham Young University and author of
Chicano While Mormon: Activism, War, and Keeping the Faith

The Book of Mormon For the Least of These is a transformative and revolutionary work that should be a stable in LDS homes across the globe. This book is a love letter to us, BIPOC (Black, Indigenous and People of Color), and it is felt with such vigor within each page. It nods to us and our struggle at the margins and reminds us that we have always been centered in sacred text. This lens shall live on and inspire great and needed transformation for the generations that are to come.

—Maybelline Alvarez-McCoy
educator, activist, and co-founder
of the LDS Legacy Conference

The Book of Mormon
For the Least of These

VOLUME 1
1 NEPHI – WORDS OF MORMON

BY COMMON CONSENT PRESS is a non-profit publisher dedicated to producing affordable, high-quality books that help define and shape the Latter-day Saint experience. BCC Press publishes books that address all aspects of Mormon life. Our mission includes finding manuscripts that will contribute to the lives of thoughtful Latter-day Saints, mentoring authors and nurturing projects to completion, and distributing important books to the Mormon audience at the lowest possible cost.

The Book of Mormon
For the Least of These

VOLUME 1
1 NEPHI – WORDS OF MORMON

By Fatimah Salleh
with Margaret Olsen Hemming

The Book of Mormon For the Least of These, volume 1: 1 Nephi–Words of Mormon
Copyright © 2020 by Fatimah Salleh and Margaret Olsen Hemming

All rights reserved. Printed in the United States of America. No part of this book may be used or reproduced in any manner whatsoever without written permission except in the case of brief quotations embodied in critical articles or reviews.

For information contact
By Common Consent Press
4062 S. Evelyn Dr.
Salt Lake City, UT 84124-2250

Cover art: "Swept Up" by Tiare Terrill (www.tiareterrillartstudio.com)
Cover design: Rosie Gochnour Serago and D Christian Harrison
Book design: Andrew Heiss

www.bccpress.org
ISBN-13: 978-1-948218-23-8

10 9 8 7 6 5 4 3 2 1

For those who seek for God and work for justice

CONTENTS

Preface	ix
Introduction	xiii
1 Nephi	1
2 Nephi	47
Jacob	103
Enos	133
Jarom	141
Omni	145
Words of Mormon	151
Conclusion	155
Acknowledgments	157

PREFACE

From the first time I started reading the Book of Mormon at 15 years old, I felt its power.

I actually cried the first time I read about Alma the younger. I rejoiced when the sons of Mosiah turned their lives around and went on their missions. And I was heartbroken at the massacre of the converted Lamanites.

I raged at Nephi's words which described a "skin of blackness" as a curse.

I wondered why the women of the wilderness journey had no voice to represent their part in the family's refugee story.

For many years I taught gospel doctrine and absolutely cherished that calling because it allowed me to delve into the scriptures. I could both learn and share in the beauty of the holy text.

After my PhD and in 2013, I started Duke Divinity School to earn a Masters in Divinity but mostly to wrestle with God and my call. As part of my course work, I learned how to exegete or critically examine scripture. The Bible has been so richly excavated for its meanings and there is no dearth of commentaries on each of the books in the Bible. As a part of exegetical work, a student of the scriptures looks to a myriad of commentaries from different lenses/perspectives to more fully understand and study the text.

This book is part of my gift back to a community that has beautifully molded and taught me about Jesus. This book is how I, as an

Preface

African American, Malaysian and Puerto Rican woman and mother, began to wrestle with the Book of Mormon in ways that call for social justice and the liberation of the oppressed.

When Margaret approached me with the invitation to work together on writing a commentary on the Book of Mormon from a social justice perspective, I could have leapt for joy. I had expressed to her several months prior how I had been wanting to do a project like this but could not find the time or energy to sit down and write it all out. For two years, Margaret and I worked together as she recorded my musings and our conversations as we started at the beginning with, "I, Nephi . . ." This book is the product of those efforts.

I must provide my ever-present disclaimer whenever I engage in scripture and theology. My ideas about God, the holy text and my faith journey are constantly under construction and revision. I have learned in these last years that I should remain open to change. So, I ask that you, the reader, offer me the grace to evolve, see things differently, and approach the work from another lens over time. For this work is dynamic and God is always on the move.

To the church and community that drew me closer to God, I am grateful to offer *The Book of Mormon for the Least of These*.

—Rev. Dr. Fatimah Salleh

A dozen years ago, I listened to a lesson in gospel doctrine class about Nephi killing Laban and I felt completely lost. At the time I was working on a graduate degree in International Peace and Conflict Resolution and thinking a great deal about the causes and effects of violence. I was also working as a case manager for the International Rescue Committee, resettling refugees in Baltimore, Maryland. The story of Nephi's family fleeing violence felt timeless and vitally important, yet the lesson—a message of unquestioning obedience—didn't speak to me. I wondered whether anyone could ever use the Book of Mormon to teach a different kind of lesson, one that felt more relevant to these issues that concerned me.

Preface

A few years ago, I met Fatimah Salleh at a Mormon women's conference. I was immediately impressed by her charisma and brilliance. Her thorough knowledge of scripture and the messages she took from it left me hungry for more of her words. We set up a regular lunch appointment and began talking about the gospel, social justice, and theology together.

During one of our first lunches, I confessed to her my long-time struggles with the Book of Mormon: I wished for more female characters, I was put off by the violence, I rarely felt inspired as I read it. She listened carefully, then shook her head and explained to me what I had been missing. She told me about how the book was about a people whose origin story was a family of refugees. She spoke about how human and fallible the prophets and writers are and how they teach us what a stumbling journey with God looks like. She explained that any holy text should engage with the reality of violence in the world, not ignore it. In our following conversations, time slipped away quickly as we dove into these ideas, building off each other's insights and creating exciting new ways of reading the Book of Mormon. In my personal scripture study, I realized that I was getting more out of reading than at any other time in my life. I was excited and inspired by these stories in ways I had never before experienced.

One morning, I awoke from a dream knowing that this work needed to be shared with the world. I had rarely felt divine direction so clearly before. At our next lunch, I presented her with the idea: we could record these conversations and then I would turn them into text. We would work our way through the Book of Mormon and publish an exegesis of the text based on ideas of anti-racism, feminism, nonviolence, and social justice.

We have met regularly, in person and online, with children in our laps and spouses walking through the room, and read the first third Book of Mormon together. We talk about every verse. For every chapter, Fatimah preaches a sermon. Ideas evolve as we discuss words and concepts. I have the privilege of listening, engaging, and writing. I have found this role of supporting Fatimah's work, helping to amplify her

Preface

voice and melding some of my ideas with hers, to be one of the most fulfilling spiritual journeys of my life. It has fundamentally changed how I read scripture and how I understand God. It is not the book I had ever anticipated writing, but I believe God knew that it was the one I needed.

—Margaret Olsen Hemming

INTRODUCTION

The strength and beauty of a holy text is that it can be read again and again, with different and new understandings and insights revealed every time. A holy text is not exhausted by a single interpretation; it compels readers to return and review, reexamine, and reinterpret. The Bible has withstood millenia of innumberable methods of understanding: orthodox, liberal, academic, literary, feminist, etc. The Book of Mormon has certainly experienced readers examining it from various points of view, including through history, literature, and orthodoxy. But a close reading of the complete book as scripture that has messages about oppression, inequality, and other issues of social justice has not been available until now. This book, the first in a trilogy, is a social justice exegesis of the first third of the Book of Mormon, from 1 Nephi to the Words of Mormon.

All forms of exegesis, or the critical interpretation of holy text, use some kind of personal interpretation, even if that personal lens goes unrecognized or unacknowledged. Unlike some other scriptural commentary, we don't pretend to be lacking bias. We wrote this book intentionally looking for messages about issues related to social justice. As we worked on this book, we specifically asked the questions: Who is present but unheard? Who is suffering and why? What kind of violence is in the background of this story? How does this call us to relieve affliction? How are these actions informed by trauma? What are the diverse ways that God is showing up in this person's life?

What are the assumptions this person is making? Is there another way to understand this story? We would never claim that this is a definitive way of reading this text, simply that it is one that has been vastly underutilized in mainstream Mormonism.

Why do we believe that this kind of interpretation—a hermeneutics of social justice—is an important missing piece to read the Book of Mormon? Simply, there is a tragic history of scripture being weaponized against populations that are already marginalized. When this happens, the radical message of the gospel, that God loves each person completely and unreservedly and calls us to do the same, is lost. Deliberately reading scripture while looking for themes of social justice provides believers with the tools to counteract that tendency. For those who experience oppression because of their race, gender, sexual orientation, socioeconomic class, or immigration status, this book provides messages of liberation. The Book of Mormon is a book of abundance. There is a richness to the text that is exciting and transformative. The narrowing of scripture so that there is one single message, one way of reading, leaves a banquet of God's word lying untouched on the table.

Critical thinkers engaging with the Book of Mormon have a great deal to struggle with: Nephi's racist epithets against his brothers, a theology of prosperity gospel, claims of God choosing sides in war, a disturbing lack of female voices or characters, and more. The exegesis provided in this book attempts to uncover some of the deeper messages that require an intense wrestle with the text. Wisdom about what a journey with God looks like is there, but sometimes goes unseen. The purpose of this book is to make the effort of seeing a little bit easier for others. More than anything, we hope that readers will feel empowered to explore the Book of Mormon in new and revolutionary ways.

As Latter-day Saints we are empowered to read and ponder the scriptures. Part of the power of sinking into scripture is that we get to let the text call to us, speak into our lives, and inspire us to be brave in our discipleship. This book is one way we have allowed the scriptures to speak. We hope our offering of this social justice lens will embolden its readers to search, ponder and pray about the many ways this holy text can transform their lives. We hope this work emboldens readers to reach for a God that calls all of us to see the oppressed and engage in the work of liberation.

A few words about how this book should be read: scriptural commentary should not be consumed all at once. We assume that the reader is immediately familiar with the text we are examining, so we recommend reading the referenced verses in the Book of Mormon first, then reading the commentary. This book should enhance your study of the Book of Mormon, so reading small sections, then sitting and pondering the concepts presented, will yield the best results. While we believe that all readers, including those new to the Book of Mormon, will enjoy this book, those who are familiar with LDS scripture will likely understand our theses most clearly. Additionally, we have chosen to leave out the portions of 2 Nephi that are quotations from Isaiah, because several social justice examinations of that text already exist.[1]

As we have described this book to people, many have asked us if we are approaching the Book of Mormon as a work of history or fiction—that is, was Nephi an actual person or did Joseph Smith create this entire story in his head? For us, that question is not particularly relevant to this project. While we will refer to characters in the book as real people, their literal existence is, for us, irrelevant to the truths we can learn from them. Truth may come to us in many forms, including stories from the past and from our brains. Indeed, we are hesitant to draw a clear line between history and fiction: all memories undergo the process of rewriting in our heads, so even if Nephi truly lived, his account of his life ought not to be read as a documentary.

---

1. We recommend Sandie Butler, David Spriggs, Nick Page, and Claire Page. *The Poverty and Justice Bible: Contemporary English Version*. Stonehill Green, Westlea, Swindon: Bible Society, 2008.

Introduction

Throughout the book, we use terms that reflect a certain kind of engagement with the Divine. We frequently refer to a "wrestle," referencing the hard and inelegant struggle to understand God or scripture. As we have worked together, we have repeatedly said out loud, "God shows up in the mess," by which we mean that mortal life is complicated, humans make terrible mistakes, and we're all deeply inadequate—but God is there for us anyway. God's grace covers us again and again, even though we don't deserve it. The Book of Mormon prophets do not shield readers from their own vulnerability. It is common for them to introduce themselves, giving their name and family background, before sharing their story. Many of them apologize in advance for their own mistakes in their accounts. The writers frequently do not skirt around times they sinned, failed, or doubted. This is a particularly human and personal book of scripture. One of the greatest gifts the Book of Mormon can give us is the understanding that even prophets are fallible humans and that a journey with God does not require flawlessness to be beautiful and valuable. This liberates us to know that we can repeatedly fail and still be called to God's work.

For this first third of the Book of Mormon, we primarily examine the origin story of the Nephites and the Lamanites. The most important theme is that this is a story of refugees who, because of their obedience to God, lost everything and journeyed into the wilderness. This section is about a family schism that will divide a nation. It includes familial abuse, violence, and fleeing into the unknown multiple times. This is a cruel, ugly, sometimes heartbreaking story. As readers, we witness it. And we also witness how God reaches out to this family, again and again.

As you read this book, we hope that you will see how the Book of Mormon calls all of us toward lives of justice work; that you will offer the people in the book and in your lives more compassion; and that you will ponder the ways in which you can liberate the oppressed. If this book helps at all in your efforts to understand your journey with God, it will have fulfilled its purpose.

1 NEPHI

1 Nephi 1:1

The first word of the first verse of the first chapter of the Book of Mormon is revolutionary for any sacred text. By using the word "I" to begin his narrative, Nephi underscores that this is his personal account. He also tells us who he is, what language he's using, and describes his relationship with God. What an introduction. A holy text where the writers name themselves allows for readers to know that scripture is embedded in the personal. While the implications of Nephi's story, as scripture, will inform a religion and give greater meaning to the gospel, it still remains one man's writings about God and his family. That one word, "I," invites a deeper understanding of Nephi's record. It allows the readers to recognize that this scripture is profoundly human, and in so doing we can witness Nephi's successes and rejoice. We can read of his hardships and weep. When he experiences great loss, we can understand his mourning. We can also see his failings and offer compassion in correction. The Book of Mormon, from its first word, is bound up in the holy and the personal. Nephi's introduction is our welcome into his complicated journey of discipleship that would become our scripture.

In the next few words, Nephi situates himself within his family unit. He begins his family's introduction in a powerful initial acknowledgment that he has "been born of goodly parents." Nephi feels it is important to name himself as the author of the text and then immediately acknowledge the goodness of his parents. These two words, "goodly parents," can be a beacon to those who struggle to raise a family through unjust and hard circumstances within their family life. What Nephi's description of his parents tells us is that while his family life would entail being driven from their homeland and rendered nearly destitute—his parents were still good. In later verses, Nephi tells the story of his family's struggles and of abuse that was so serious that it not only ripped apart his immediate family, but also had consequences that rippled down through generations and ended in the total destruction of a civilization. Here is a person who has been through so much, suffered so much within his family, and he still calls his parents good. In these few choice words, "goodly parents," Nephi honors Lehi and Sariah.[1]

1 Nephi 1:3

After introducing himself and his parentage, Nephi offers a caveat to his scriptural work: "I make [this record] of mine own hand; and I make it according to my knowledge." He says, right at the beginning where it can't be missed, "If there are mistakes here, they are my own." From the beginning, Nephi sets a standard for the Book of Mormon prophets, who frequently acknowledge any mistakes in their accounts. Here, Nephi declares his inherent fallibility as a prophet. He demonstrates both humility and transparency. Upfront and early in the text, Nephi underlines the limits of his own knowledge. At the time of this writing, later in his life, Nephi has an unusual breadth and depth of understanding about the world. He's seen visions of the

---

1. During the creation, every so often God looked over what had been created and said, "This is good," while still knowing that at times it wouldn't be so good. The earth that God created would shake and destroy, the water would flood and suffocate, the plants would cause sickness and death, the animals would turn violent, and humans would do unspeakably horrific things to one another. And yet, in our very existence, God says we are good. Nephi sees in this way as well.

future of the world. But he chooses to emphasize that his knowledge is limited and holds boundaries. And yet, even as Nephi says that his knowledge is limited and that a perfect God cannot be perfectly rendered with imperfect hands, he still obeys God and tells his story.

This happens again and again in the Book of Mormon. Prophets and/or writers announce themselves at the beginning of their writing. Multiple prophets of the Book of Mormon emphasize that any faults in the text are their fault, not God's—in essence saying, "This is my experience. This is how God moved with me. This was my community. It wasn't perfect, but God still spoke to us." This is how a holy text leaves space for grace in human error.

1 Nephi 1:20

In the very first chapter, Nephi and his family became refugees. This is an important moment in the story. Nephi tells us that his people have a history of killing the prophets because we need to know that his family is in real and present danger. They have to leave their country under threat of violence. This is a story of refugees.

What do we do with the word "chosen" in this verse? The Bible often cites the Hebrews as declaring themselves God's chosen people, and Nephi's use of the word here seems deliberate. When there's a chosen family within a "chosen" people, the word, as typically understood, seems less than useful. But in this verse, "chosenness" is not about being specially singled out by God. Nephi describes chosenness as a natural result of a person's faith, not as an arbitrary label: "All those whom he hath chosen, because of their faith." So, according to Nephi, chosenness is more about one's deliberate faith and their choice to be in relationship with God. Here chosenness is not linked to ethnicity and/or culture.

This idea is repeated a chapter later, after Nephi makes his well-known declaration that he "will go and do the things which the Lord hath commanded," and Lehi responds with being exceedingly glad, "for he knew that [Nephi] had been blessed of the Lord."[2] In Lehi's eyes, Nephi's bold statement of faith is evidence of God's blessing. Faith is, in itself, chosenness and a blessing. It is faith, in this case, that sets Nephi apart.

What if chosenness is more about choosing God than about ancestral lineage? What if chosenness is about being a recipient of God's tender mercies and being made mighty enough to do hard things and be delivered?

Chosenness is highly problematic in scripture and theology. For if there is a chosen then there must be an unchosen. Any theology that would bifurcate and divide God's children into the favored and unfavored can be a destructive and harmful mindset. What purpose does it serve to name one's people, or any people, chosen over another?

Within scripture, the terminology and the use of the word "chosen" needs careful examination and revaluation as to how it is used in today's church doctrine and dialogue. The doctrine of the chosen easily lends itself to racism, xenophobia, discriminaiton and prejudice. In this way, the idea of a chosen children of God can be considered a gateway to social and cultural evils. While some may suggest that the complete eradication of the idea of chosenness is necessary to an inclusive theology, Nephi's description offers a more expansive view.

Nephi recaptures the idea of chosenness and broadens its definition. The people of Jerusalem, a society that had claimed the title of chosenness, threatened Lehi's life, endangering Nephi's entire family and forcing them into the wilderness. Nephi's lived experience undermines the traditional idea of what chosenness looks like. To claim chosenness, he has to redefine it in a way that encapsulates his family's struggle and journey. So he sculpts a definition of chosen as one who willingly enters into a faith journey with the Divine, one who has felt the tender mercies of the Lord, one who has been empowered to survive the harshness and unfairness of this life.

---

2. 1 Nephi 3: 7–8

The final sentence is a beautiful display of the paradoxes that the Book of Mormon will undertake to explore. Nephi has just stated that his family is fleeing for their lives because his father has spoken God's word. His family is about to walk away from all their material goods and walk into a harrowing wilderness journey as refugees. Yet still, Nephi sees God's tender mercies. He sees God choosing them and they are choosing God. In the same breath, Nephi speaks of the persecution and the threat of death, as the family's lives are saved only through God's deliverance. That flips the traditional understanding of deliverance on its head. Nephi begins his story by setting up readers for just how contradictory his story is going to look. The story here looks like a kind of reverse Exodus, with Lehi's family abandoning prosperity instead of fleeing enslavement, and yet also walking into the wilderness and the unknown.

1 Nephi 2:4

Nephi gives an itemized list of the riches that they left behind, making it clear that walking away from those nice things was hard for him. He takes the time to write out the list, indicating the meaning that their wealth played in his life at the time. This could not have been an easy sacrifice for Nephi. He also notes that they took only what was necessary. And the first thing that was necessary was each other.[3] At the same time, the choice to take everyone lays the groundwork for what is arguably their greatest struggle in the wilderness. While they fled the threats of external communal violence, they still brought internal familial violence with them.

This text challenges us to simultaneously look with open eyes at abuse and violence, while also suspending our judgment of those who possibly could have prevented it. We don't know the full story. We don't know why Lehi and Sariah couldn't or wouldn't protect

---

3. They took each other. In some way in our lives, we are all called on a journey with God. And we will need the wisdom to leave the gold and silver, and take each other. The first step of the journey is just seeing each and taking each other along.

their younger sons better. We only know that God tells Lehi to take his family into the wilderness, and that's what he does. But just because we don't have the answers doesn't mean we shouldn't raise the questions. Nephi's narrative pushes us toward discomfort with questions we cannot answer.

1 Nephi 2:6–10

This is the first of many moments in the Book of Mormon when land is tied to the spiritual condition of its inhabitants. Land is a major character in traditional sacred text.[4] Later in the Book of Mormon, we'll see instances where the land responds to unrighteousness—where there is so much violence perpetrated that the land is abandoned and becomes a wasteland. It's worth asking throughout the book what the land is representing and how both the people and the prophets are naming and moving in the land.

While it's possible to read this section as a scolding of Laman and Lemuel, it's also possible to read it as the ultimate show of parental hope. Lehi sees a beautiful river, a lovely valley, and he thinks of his sons. Lehi's love for his sons shows in his inclination to see something good and connect it to a child who is struggling. His hope and encouragement as he invokes his blessing for them is palpable saying, "You can do this. You can be a good man. Your life can flow into righteousness."

1 Nephi 2:11

Here we find the key sentence to what this family is called to do: "to leave the land of their inheritance."[5] Laman and Lemuel struggle because they have to leave the land of their inheritance and walk

---

4. Dr. Anathea Portier-Young taught this concept of land as a major character in her Old Testament course at Duke Divinity School in Fall 2013.
5. Privilege is the things that you have through inheritance. You have those things because you were born where you were born; you didn't necessarily do anything to earn them. For Laman and Lemuel, this is their gold, silver, and precious things.

into the wilderness, a space that is unknown and uncomfortable.[6] For Laman and Lamuel, it may be difficult to imagine a God that would ask them to forsake their status and riches in exchange for instability and hardship. The Book of Mormon starts with the story of an immigrant family who left their means/privilege/social status and risked their lives for the wilderness. One key to the story is in Lehi knowing a worse fate awaited him and his family if they stayed. This verse depicts how hard it can be to follow a "visionary person."

1 Nephi 2:12

Again and again throughout scripture, God calls the younger sibling to lead the elder ones.[7] This is always challenging for the older brothers. They have the birthright and the authority. By religious and cultural standards, they are the ones who ought to lead. Society confirms their power and leadership within the familial structure. Why does God call the younger sibling? We're working with a gospel that frequently overturns cultural standards. We're also working within a gospel where the last shall be first. Along with several others, this text addresses the social rules about who has authority, who is important, and whose voices ought to lead us, but the gospel as it's lived out does not always adhere to, in fact often defies, societal and cultural norms. God reminds us again and again that God will call on those who have little to no social standing to be spiritual leaders.[8]

---

6. Laman and Lemuel value their privilege over God's commandments. It is a hard commandment to forsake one's wealth and material goods for the wilderness of a refugee life. It is a commandment of seismic proportions to lay down our means and follow God's command.

7. Some Biblical examples include Abel and Cain; Isaac and Ishmael; Jacob and Esau; Joseph and his brothers; Moses and Aaron; and David and Eliab.

8. If our social and religious structures consistently call those who we expect to be called into positions of leadership, then we can certainly miss important voices within our community and wards. In overlooking the proverbial younger siblings, we risk not hearing the necessary perspectives of our brothers and sisters whose social standing does not offer a platform for their words.

1 Nephi 2:16–19

Nephi implies that there was a time that he did not fully believe. If his heart had to be softened, then there was a time that his heart was hardened. We can see that in the earlier text as well, when Nephi catalogues the list of valuables that the family lost when they fled Jerusalem.[9] We can see from his writing that he struggled with following his father into the wilderness. Understandably, he appears to join Laman and Lamuel in feeling the loss of their home and wealth. But this verse is where Nephi separates himself from his older brothers. It's not that he never struggled to believe or that he never had doubts. What separates him is that he goes to God with those struggles and doubts. When he gets his answer, Nephi goes back and tells Laman and Lemuel to also engage and ask God. As far as we can tell from the text, they do not go to God. The difference between the brothers is not whether they have doubts but their willingness to bring their questions to God. God does not condemn them for having doubts or questions. A person seeking discipleship will not push away those feelings, but instead go to God with them.

In verse 19, the Lord blesses Nephi for his faith. What did that faith look like? Nephi diligently sought God. Faith is a work of seeking. The two key pieces to Nephi's faith is that it was diligent and that he had lowliness of heart. This verse reveals that Nephi didn't go to God once and immediately get a revelation. He doesn't write about all the times he prayed and didn't get an answer, but we can conclude that they happened because Nephi kept seeking God's answers. Nephi had to struggle. He had to come to God repeatedly, with the humility to receive the answer. This verse establishes that faith and works are not necessarily separate. Faith, in and of itself, requires persistence and hard work.[10]

---

9. 1 Nephi 2:4

10. Why was lowliness of heart a key part of receiving revelation? The answer is in the revelation itself. We have to buttress our questioning with true humility because that allows us to be ready to accept whatever answer will come, even if it's not the

God gives Nephi one bit of comfort along with a devastating answer to Nephi's prayer. When God tells Nephi that Laman and Lemuel will rebel, God says, "They rebel against me too." God is telling Nephi that, when someone is abused, God is abused too. This is a beautiful inversion of the Matthew 25 scripture, when Christ tells his followers that if we offer food, shelter, or comfort to the needy, we offer it to Him as well.[11] When Laman and Lemuel beat Nephi with a rod, God is beaten too.[12] God names Nephi's trials first—"thy brethren shall rebel against thee"—and then God puts Godself in the same camp—"they shall rebel against me." The answer to Nephi's prayer is that Nephi's life is going to get harder. But God says: they do it to me too. Get ready, it's going to get worse, and I'm with you.

1 Nephi 3:11-27

After casting lots, Laman goes to retrieve the records from Laban, only to be kicked out, called a robber and threatened with death. He flees for his life and is ready to give up the mission. Nephi suggests that the brothers retrieve their wealth and offer it up to Laban in exchange for the plates. Nephi's proposal tells us that the family truly left behind their valuables—they fled for their lives and took only what could be used for their survival. Because Lehi was obedient, the entire family had to leave behind their home, wealth, status and way of life. This important detail needs to be underscored. This family left almost everything.

---

answer we want or expect. The answer, in Nephi's case, was not, "Go back to your land, you're safe now" or "It will be an easy journey to the promised land." The answer Nephi receives is that his brothers will rebel against him and that the coming journey will be harder than he ever dreamed. Humility has to be present for a disciple to be capable of receiving an answer like that. When we go to God with our questioning, diligence and humility will allow us to find an answer. Often, that answer will not be the one for which we hoped.

11. Matthew 25
12. Alma 7:11

Lehi's sons are trying to follow God's commandments and the direction of their father, the prophet. They need the record of their people, the same people they were fleeing due to impending violence. The record is so valuable that not only are they willing to trade all their wealth in exchange for them, they are willing to risk their lives by returning to their community. The record is important because it tells their story, a story that needs passing on and preservation for future generations. From this, we understand the infinite value of knowing one's history and having a knowledge of God's dealings with your people.[13]

1 Nephi 3: 28–31

These are some of the most disturbing verses in Nephi's record. The boldness with which he describes the abuse, the way Laman and Lemuel turn so rapidly to rage, and the limited help from the angel are all difficult to read and digest.

The fact that the angel doesn't stop the situation until after Nephi and Sam have been beaten with a rod leaves the reader struggling with the Problem of Evil—the question of why an omnipotent and loving God allows terrible things to happen. In this case, the need for human agency doesn't give enough of an answer, as the angel does eventually stop the abuse and tells Laman and Lemuel to return to Jerusalem. So if there will be divine interference, why doesn't God simply stop the abuse sooner? Why not get involved when they are enacting the verbal and emotional abuse? God rescues Nephi and Sam, but it feels late. The wrestle with the text may be with a God who appears to let things go too far. Without an explanation for why

---

13. Although God gives them this commandment, God does not ever spell out how to do it or stop them from failing in their attempts. God allows for trial and error, even when we're directly following commandments and acting in faith. We will be asked to do things by God that we don't even want to do in the first place, then we'll try to be obedient, and then we will still fail. Sometimes it will not make human sense. It will only make God sense.

God waits to protect Nephi and Sam, we are left with sitting with that discomfort and thinking about what it means for us when God seems to refrain from stopping terrible pain in the world. The text doesn't provide us with an easy answer.[14]

1 Nephi 4:5–18

Perhaps no other story in the Book of Mormon poses a more difficult ethical dilemma than Nephi killing Laban. On the one hand, the Holy Spirit repeatedly speaks to Nephi, telling him that this is the way to protect Nephi's family and descendants from a man who has repeatedly tried to murder him and his brothers. On the other hand, Nephi is stealing property and murdering someone who is unprotected and physically weak. Whatever choice he makes, Nephi must break a commandment—either God's word in scripture or God's word to Nephi individually. We can see Nephi's understanding of his dilemma in the way that he argues back and forth inside himself. He cites scripture, particularly the Law of Moses and the Ten Commandments. In the end, Nephi chooses to "obey the spirit" and kill Laban.

Nephi's wrestle with the Spirit and scripture exemplifies how scripture can contradict itself. Commandments are not always coherent—they are sometimes in tension, forcing us to navigate the best path in our own circumstances and with the guidance of the Spirit. Scripture writers tell of numerous situations in which prophets are told to do something that breaks one commandment in order

---

14. When the angel does show up, it is with a question: "Why do ye smite your younger brother with a rod?" We don't know from the text whether Laman and Lemuel answer that question. Possibly they don't answer it. Possibly Nephi chooses to omit their answer, refusing to give them a voice in a moment when they are abusing him and when he knows that the abuse will continue. Regardless, the question is vital for anyone who acts in anger: Why am I doing this? Why do I react this way? What is deep in me that is sparking this action? The angel's question provides Laman and Lemuel with the opportunity to examine and change their behavior, but they choose to not take it.

to obey another.¹⁵ Similarly, we cannot make the claim that life is as simple as following the commandments and/or following scripture. As Nephi shows, life with God and scripture is complex.

However, there is still a case that Nephi made a poor decision. The evidence is in the violence that brackets the killing of Laban. Before Laban's death, Nephi's family experiences the direct threat of violence and death. They are forced to leave their home and become refugees in the wilderness. Soon after that, Laman and then Nephi have to run for their lives to avoid Laban's attempts to kill them. Immediately before Laban's death, Nephi is seriously abused by his brothers. The fact that those who experience violence often act in violence toward others is well-documented. The trauma of being forced from their home and the stress of Laban's attacks may very well have subconsciously influenced Laman and Lemuel's treatment of Nephi and Sam. In any case, Nephi has been the victim of serious physical and emotional violence in just the last few days. It is easy to believe that he is not in a healthy emotional state in which he could make clear decisions, particularly under heavy stress and in a short period of time. We know that when someone experiences powerlessness in his/her life through being a repeated victim of violence, that person sometimes sees violence as the only way to regain a sense of control. Acting in violence allows a person to engage in a potent myth—one that permits that person to make sense of chaos and seemingly purposeless struggle and pain.¹⁶ Nephi's action should not be taken out of context of the abuse, pain, and terror that he has recently endured.

In the end, the reader's role is not to judge Nephi's choice, but rather to empathize with his suffering and consider how we can use God's voice to navigate the challenging choices we make in our own lives. Many of us will, at some point, face conflicting command-

---

15. For example, Eve, Abraham, and Nephi all had to privilege one commandment over another.
16. Chris Hedges, *War is a Force That Gives Us Meaning* (New York, Anchor, 2002), 23.

ments or prophetic direction that conflicts with personal revelation. Nephi's actions indicate that the influence of the Holy Ghost ought to serve as the most important factor in making decisions for our own personal journeys.

There is one more episode of violence in this chapter that warrants review and perhaps also reflects on our understanding of Nephi's murder of Laban, and that is in the following verses, in which Nephi threatens Zoram.

1 Nephi 4: 20-35

Although Nephi has internally struggled with whether to kill Laban and makes a point to share his struggle with the reader, he seems to have no compunction at all with threatening the life of Laban's servant, Zoram. Yet killing Zoram would have been a far more immoral action. Laban had threatened Nephi's life and his brothers. It's possible that in order to obtain the plates and survive, Nephi had to kill Laban. But Zoram is an innocent bystander who happens to be in the wrong place at the wrong time. There are many ways Nephi could have creatively gotten rid of him. Zoram believed that Nephi was Laban and Nephi could have simply ordered him away. Nephi's jump from agonizing over killing Laban to casually "seizing" Zoram and threatening Zoram's life is disturbing. It is possible that the murder has opened up Nephi to violence and killing someone no longer seems impossible. It's also possible that Nephi sees Zoram, a servant, in a different light than he sees Laban, a wealthy landowner. It is impossible for us to know, but Nephi's sudden change in how he talks about committing violence against someone is striking. Because Nephi has killed a man, Zoram now poses an even greater threat to him and his family. He could expose Nephi, and have their clan pursued and apprehended. It may be that Nephi's ultimatum to Zoram represented the only option he could see.

Nephi tells a narrative where the conflict is resolved peacefully and Zoram willingly goes with the family into the wilderness. But when the choice is between death and something else, it's not a real choice. Zoram is forced to leave his home and become a refugee at the hand of Nephi, an echo of the earlier story of what Nephi and his family suffered. Is Nephi as guilty as the residents of Jerusalem, who forced his family into the wilderness? While Nephi doesn't examine the violence he perpetrates here, the text later gives us evidence that Zoram may have certainly experienced this event differently from Nephi's perspective. In Alma 54:23, Ammaron, king of the Lamanites, writes a letter of war to Moroni. He writes, "Behold, I am Ammaron, and a descendant of Zoram, whom your fathers pressed and brought out of Jerusalem." Zoram's descendants have received a different narrative from what we're given in Nephi's book. While the basic facts are the same, the interpretation is very different. Some of Zoram's family strongly resented being forced out of Jerusalem, to the point that many generations later, Ammaron identifies himself by invoking this moment that Nephi writes of so casually. It is hard to tell where the truth lies—readers cannot know whether Zoram told his children a bitter story of violence or whether Zoram's descendants recreated the story in a new way. Regardless, Nephi's interaction with Zoram has much greater significance than it seems to have in the moment. Nephi's violence against Zoram has repercussions for many generations to come. While readers have traditionally spent more time examining Nephi's violence toward Laban, it is the violence toward Zoram that perhaps warrants more study. We could begin with questions such as, "When is violence justified? Does murdering Laban desensitize Nephi to violence? What does it mean for us, as readers, that we never get Zoram's perspective on this incident? Why do the perspectives of those who are present but silent matter?"

1 Nephi 5:2–9

These verses about Sariah's anguish make up one of the only sections we have about this woman, wife and mother. In most of the rest of the story, she is mentioned in passing, as someone who is present but is not integrally woven into the narrative. These verses are our opportunity to understand her experience. Too often, this section is read or taught as a criticism of Sariah—that she is faithless or complaining. But she has already shown extraordinary faith in leaving her home and walking into the wilderness. A close reading of these verses reveals a woman of great heart on a journey with God.

It's hard for any of us to imagine how we would respond in Sariah's situation. Her four sons have left and she believes that they are dead. Her fears for her children are not unfounded. As she and Lehi wait in the wilderness, it feels like the only future for them is death. She has lost her homeland, probably her extended family and friends she's known her whole life, she thinks she has lost her children, and she believes she will perish in the wilderness.

When Sariah describes her losses, it sounds different from when Nephi lists the gold and silver and precious things, or when Laman and Lemuel complain about the wealth and comfort they left behind.[17] Sariah refers to the loss of "the land of our inheritance." For the ancient Israelites, land was community, history, identity, and religion all in one. It was their birthright from God and the place where their people belonged. Sariah is not grieving their material wealth. She is grieving her whole sense of self and her people. We should not condemn a grief that is born of real suffering and vulnerability.

Lehi's response to Sariah's anguish is beautiful. He comforts her. There is no rebuke here. He agrees with her—"I know I am visionary man"—and we can read this cry as his own admission of feeling the burden of what he has asked from his family. In this moment in their marriage—a moment of grief, loss, and conflict—there is comfort. Lehi doesn't chide her by saying she needs a stronger testimony or more faith. He doesn't tell her she's not doing enough or turn her anger back on her. He comforts her.

It's also beautiful to note that Nephi wasn't present to witness this scene, which means that Lehi and Sariah must have shared it

---

17. 1 Nephi 2:11

with their children later. They didn't have to share this story of grief and anger, nor did Nephi have to make a record of it. They chose to share a moment of an authentic wrestle with doubt, fear, and loss. Once again, this record is one of imperfect, struggling people who are on a journey with God.

Lehi and Sariah must have also shared with their sons how Lehi comforted his wife. What a thing for a son to know that in a moment of conflict, his father offered comfort to his mother. For a child to write that in text, to testify of times when his family clung to each other in comfort, that's a powerful and vulnerable moment. Rather than condemning Sariah for her struggle, Lehi leads his family in encircling her in comfort and love. The text tells us that "their joy was full." In her time of need, Sariah becomes the center of the family universe. God cared about her comfort and joy.

How does Sariah respond to this comforting and the return of her sons? "Now I know of a surety." Now she knows. Like Nephi before, writing that he needed his heart to be softened, this phrase reveals that Sariah's testimony of their call to the wilderness was not so sure. Now she knows. But there's this beautiful weaving together of comfort, joy, and faith. While Laman and Lemuel are able to witness an angel without it confirming their faith, the safety of Sariah's children confirms her faith. She walks a different path from the men in this family. We don't have a record of her speaking with angels or having visions. What she needs for her faith in this moment is for her children to return to her safely. Through that comfort, her joy is made full and then her testimony strengthens. For this woman, joy, faith, and comfort are all wrapped up together during a time of hardship and sacrifice. Her conversion is built just a little differently, and God knows it.

The story culminates with the family making sacrifices and giving thanks. It's good to remember that the sacrifices they are burning are from the rations they have taken with them into the wilderness. They are still refugees, living in tents. Their joy and gratitude is still wrapped up in grief and loss. For this family, following God will always be complex.

1 Nephi 5:14–16

Most of the remainder of this chapter is Lehi's exploration of the plates that came from Laban. It is worth noting the time that this takes in the record, as well as the fact that this family was willing to risk their lives to have their ancestral record. This is in keeping with LDS belief in the crucial importance of family records and of knowing your ancestral history. For those populations who experienced the systemic erasure of their culture and language, this section can be painful. So much is lost, so much is stripped away from a people, when they are forcibly torn from their families and their land. If having ancestral records was critical for Lehi's family in building a new community in a new land, then we can see how much is lost to a people separated from their people, records, and land. More was lost at the slave auction block than freedom and dignity. The sin is not just against the individual, but against generations of people. Anyone who strips another person of their ability to root themselves in history has harmed not just one person, but generations of people.

1 Nephi 7:19

Ishmael's wife, daughter, and son are literally the unnamed heroes of this chapter. Laman and Lemuel are once again falling into their patterns of rage and abuse. Nephi prays for protection. And these three people stand up, putting their bodies between Nephi and his brothers. They have just witnessed these men bind up Nephi and threaten to leave him to die in the wilderness. Given Laman and Lemuel's propensity for violence, there is no reason for Ishmael's family members to think that their advocacy for Nephi would end without physical consequences. Yet, these three show extraordinary courage and exemplify the behavior of those who wish to protect vulnerable and hurting people. In addition, they show themselves to be peacemakers, able to say the words that stop Laman and Lemuel's abuse. Given their great show of spiritual strength and wisdom, it is confusing and unfortunate that they go unnamed.

1 Nephi 8

Much has been written about this chapter and the meaning it gives to LDS doctrine. When Lehi tastes of the fruit or Love of God, he is filled with "exceedingly great joy." What a beautiful revelation it is to know that when one partakes and knows that they are loved by God, they are filled with immense joy. In his joy, Lehi looks for his family. Something profound happens the moment Lehi partakes of God's love, an immediate reaction to look for his loved ones. He wants them to feel this love, experience the joy he's feeling. God's love is tied to a joy that longs to be shared. And for this immigrant, this displaced and uprooted prophet, this joy that stems from God's love is not to be experienced alone. Perhaps the origin of missionary work is simple: I have felt God's love and know what joy it brings. In turn, this conjures a deep desire that others share in that profound love. It is no coincidence that the iron rod or the Word of God would lead one to partake of God's love. The Word of God speaks to God's love and should lead us to know just how precious and loved we all are are as children of God. One of the divine purposes of the Word of God is that it will lead us to experience the immense joy of knowing we are loved by God.

This chapter should allow us to envision how God shows up in places we might think of as desolate or wicked. God is at work in the spacious building. God is also at the river, making every attempt to pull out those who are drowning. God is in the mists of darkness, beckoning people to light. Calls to serve God through helping others burst forth from the building, the river, and all along the strait and narrow path. All the spaces which are evil, prideful, or seemingly lost are the spaces where God can still be at work. Prophets and disciples are called to every space, including some of the darkest ones. Jesus taught that "they that are whole have no need of the physician, but they that are sick: I came not to call the righteous, but sinners to repentance."[18]

Our bodies may be limited to physical space, but we must think beyond that. God's word allows us to hold on to the Divine and simultaneously wander in the mists of darkness, seeking our loved ones and knowing how to return home. If we are called to find the lost sheep, then our grip on the iron rod must become a tether, a way to stay grounded while also doing the work.

1 Nephi 9:5

Nephi deserves acknowledgement here for doing painstaking work and not receiving an answer about the purpose of the other plates. We know that Nephi is a seeker—he has already repeatedly gone to God for answers and will do so again in the following chapters—so it's fair to infer that he asked God about the purpose. In other cases, God gives all the explanation that Nephi could ask for and more. In this chapter, no explanation is given. Although Nephi is a prophet, the answer he gets is, "You don't get to know that right now." Nephi is not only willing to accept that answer and still do the work, he's also willing to admit in this record that he doesn't know all of God's mysteries and that sometimes God's answers leave him still in the unknowing.

1 Nephi 10:17–19

"I, Nephi, was desirous also that I might see, and hear, and know of these things." This is the second time that Nephi writes that someone has told him something important and he has the desire to have it confirmed through his own spiritual experience. Rather than passively accepting the truth that he hears, he actively searches out his own experience and has truth erupt all around him. We should

---

18. Mark 2:17

not miss the verbs he uses: see, hear, and know. He's looking for an immersive experience. He wants to be overwhelmed with a holistic sensory overload of the Spirit. He wants it to penetrate his being. Nephi makes is clear again and again that he will go to God and say, "I want to know." We know from this chapter that he sometimes receives knowledge beyond what he could imagine. We know from 9:5 that sometimes he does not, but that he continues to seek. The unknowing and the knowing are encased together, different parts of the same deep relationship with God.

Nephi also tells us in this verse that "all those who diligently seek him" will receive revelation. Of all the descriptions we could use for Nephi, "diligent seeker" may be the most appropriate. He repeats the phrase in verse 19: "For he that diligently seeketh shall find; and the mysteries of God shall be unfolded unto them." To receive truth and understand the mysteries of God is an unfolding process. When a map is being unfolded, some things stay hidden while some things are laid open. Nephi's best example for us is as someone who works hard for spiritual knowledge and growth.

1 Nephi 11:1

Latter-day Saints often answer the question of how the Spirit speaks by invoking the scriptural language of the "still small voice."[19] Here, Nephi experiences the Spirit in a completely different way. Nephi is "caught away," seemingly experiencing an out-of-body vision with a Spirit who is vigorous and passionate. Of the 103 exclamation points in the entire Book of Mormon, twelve of them come from this revelation, as the Spirit shouts again and again at Nephi to *Look!* at the vision. It is worth remembering that communication from God is as wildly diverse as God's children and that we should avoid limiting the ways in which the Spirit can communicate, lest we not hear everything that the Spirit is saying. God may speak in a whisper. God

---

19. 1 Kings 19:12

and God's angels may speak in a shout. To speak loudly can also be the language of reverence and worship.

1 Nephi 11:2–4

Just as when an angel appeared to the four brothers outside of Jerusalem as they tried to get the plates from Laban, the first words from the Spirit are a question, not an answer: "Behold, what desirest thou?" and "Believest thou that thy father saw the tree of which he hath spoken?" We should not be surprised if a holy response to our questions contains more questions. In fact, the best questions often lead to more good questions. We see this in the New Testament in Jesus' discussions: when someone asks a question, he often responds with another question. Don't let that stop your seeking. A question as a response may be the answer we need.

The rest of this chapter is full of witnessing God. The Spirit reminds Nephi again and again to truly see Christ, to witness God's miracles. The most foundational action for discipleship is observing God's work. Seeing and hearing through spiritual eyes and ears is a spiritual practice. Disciples notice how God shows up in the world around them. Before we can do anything else, we must follow the Spirit's direction to look. And not just look, but *look!* and then *look!* again. Nephi's revelation shows how questions follow questions, how the knowing and the unknowing are wrapped up together, and how looking is a crucial component to gaining our testimony.

1 Nephi 12:19–21

Prophetic call is never easy, but the burden of Nephi's vision in verses 19–20 is almost unimaginable. Nephi suffers under the abuse of his brothers. They mock, beat, and bind him repeatedly. In this vision, he finds out that not only will he never reach a resolution with them, but that hundreds of years of conflict will ensue, ending only when his brothers' descendants destroy Nephi's descendants. It is hard to imagine the shock and pain that this knowledge would create. It prompts the question of why God would find this information necessary or good for Nephi to know. Sharing this vision when Nephi is struggling to survive in the wilderness, living with brothers who have harmed him so deeply, seems cruel. Yet it may serve an important purpose.

Humans sometimes have a tendency toward tribalism, and Nephi comes from a culture that was particularly rooted in that way of life. Since at least the time of Abraham, the Hebrew people had understood biological descendancy as foundational in their relationship to God. The promise of innumerable descendants was part of their covenant and promise. These verses expose Nephi's extremely narrow definition of lineage. He may not see his brothers' descendants as his kin, although those people are also the descendants of Abraham and are children of the covenant. But Nephi is ready to adopt a division, seeing the conflict as one between separate peoples instead of within a family.

In seeing the destruction of his direct descendants, Nephi is challenged to let go of his attachment to his specific blood lineage. He knows from almost the very beginning of his prophetic call that his personal and individual biological legacy will end. In the face of that knowledge, he could curse God for failing to follow through with covenants. Or, he could let go of his old way of thinking of lineage as strictly biological. The value of Nephi's record will not be for his literal descendants. His lineage will die out. His record is for the human race, including the Lamanites, including the Gentiles, including all people. Nephi must step out of tribalism and embrace a wider vision of family.

Perhaps, for all of us, there has to be a death of what we think of as our lineage. For many of us, this is not about a biological legacy. What will continue is our community and brother/sisterhood and that which binds us as believers and truth-tellers. We must all face the question of who we consider to be our people and who we do not. Maybe Nephi receives this vision as a prompt from God, as a push toward understanding that he will have to let go of this idea of biological legacy and covenant, and adopt a wider vision of who might be considered his people.[20]

It is also worth remembering that Nephi's record of his vision means that all the following Nephite prophets also know what will eventually happen to their people. As they teach and engage in missionary work, they know that the Nephites will die out.[21] There are hopeful stretches in the Book of Mormon, periods of time where people are living good lives, working for peace, and creating good community. Yet still the writers of the Book of Mormon know that those periods of peace are fleeting. Because of Nephi's vision, they know that destruction will eventually follow. There's something powerful in their continued faith in the face of that knowledge.

---

20. If we don't understand that the gospel is counter-cultural, we are going to have a hard time recognizing how Christ is butting up against cultural norms and asking us to question our own assumptions. That aspect of Christ is hard to reckon with because it shatters so much of how we understand the world and replaces it with something broader and deeper than we could have anticipated. In the case of this vision, God is overturning the idea of tribalism and who is considered family. Nephi may not fully understand that message, but it is an essential theme to the rest of the Book of Mormon. In the landscape of the Book of Mormon, we'll see this thread of division and brother/sisterhood repeatedly. All through this book, prophets are asked to walk away from tribalism and prejudice. They will be challenged to understand that although the Nephites and the Lamanites are disconnected now, ultimately their journey is fundamentally interwoven. The prophets succeed and fail to varying degrees—Enos asks God for a promise that the Lamanites will someday receive the Book of Mormon (Enos 1:16) and Moroni continues the record after the destruction of the Nephites in the hopes that it will be helpful to the Lamanites (Moroni 1:4). On the other hand, Nephi sets an example of violent conflict that generations of Nephite leaders will follow (2 Nephi 5:14).

21. What does that say about their call? No matter what the ultimate outcome is, doing the work of God still matters in the moment. The individual soul is of infinite worth in itself, not just for its potential to produce lineage. And the future may not look like what you want, but you still have to do the work. That may feel hopeless, but Latinx theologian Miguel A. de la Torre claims that hopelessness may be exactly where we need to be in order to take the risks we need to take for God (see Jessica Wood, "Resurrecting a Badass Christianity: De La Torre speaks for Matthew Simpson Lecture," *The Simpsonian*, Dec. 9, 2019).

1 Nephi 12:22–23

These words are painful to read, which is a clue to how we should read them. We are getting words coming out of Nephi's mouth when he is in deep grief. He is also angry. He is deeply devastated by what he has seen of the future of his descendants. Not only will he not see justice in this life but his descendants will face endless war and finally be wiped out. Prophets are human. They suffer and experience frustration and anger. We have to let Nephi grieve, hold space for him as he experiences one of the darkest moments of his life. He is rightfully upset with what he's just experienced. He is wounded by his brothers. This is a time when we have to let scripture be a description, not a prescription, of peoples' walks with God. The fact that scripture holds the whole spectrum of humans' relationships with God makes it more useful and holy for us, not less. The Bible has an entire book called Lamentations—maybe this section, and a few others that will follow it, is best thought of as part of Nephi's lament.

These verses and the highly charged words that come from Nephi issue the reader two challenges: to hold space for Nephi's grief and give his humanity some compassion. Don't redact the words, don't strip them, don't ignore them. Allow Nephi his anger, remembering that he was going through such a hard and devastating season. At the same time, we must not take his angry, destructive words and make them doctrine. It is tragic that these words, and others that Nephi will use to describe the Lamanites,[22] have been historically used by the LDS Church and its members to justify racism. There is no justification for weaponizing this scriptural text as a means of explaining church policy and church practices. These words, stemming from a man in deep pain and anguish, can help us to more fully understand how trauma can manifest itself, but any other use can be run counter to doctrine etc.

---

22. 2 Nephi 5:21–24, among others

We need to allow prophets human complexity. When we do not let our prophets be people, we strip them of the human journey and fail to recognize how life and its unwieldy hardships can impact them and their ministry. This is the spiritual challenge: listen, hold space for Nephi, understand the complexity of who he is and what he's been through, and leave the words there. Do not elevate these words to a position of doctrine. That doesn't mean simply ignoring them or pretending that they are not part of the text. It is a higher law: we must be readers of compassion who engage in relationship with the writer and at the same time are fully able to name harmful and destructive dialogue.

1 Nephi 13:4-9

Readers may limit themselves through a too narrow definition of the word "church" here. In looking for a formal structure, an organized religion with buildings and clergy, may lead to unfortunate interpretations. Bruce R. McConkie infamously labeled the Catholic Church as the great and abominable church.[23] CES teachers have described the great and abominable church as being anything that isn't the LDS Church.[24] More recently, Church teachings have adopted a softer tone, saying that the great and abominable church is any church that leads people away from God. Scripture tells us that when two or three people are gathered in God's name, God is with them.[25] So a church does not require organization or structures to be a church. When people come together in community and worship, that is church. We need not be limited by the connotation of the word church. A church may be fluid, flexible, and informal.

---

23. Bruce R. McConkie, *Mormon Doctrine* [1st edition]. Salt Lake City: Bookcraft, 1958.
24. This is the interpretation Margaret Olsen was given in seminary classes in Lehi, Utah in 2000.
25. Matthew 18:20

Instead of looking for a formal church, to find the great and abominable church we need to closely examine how the angel defines this church. The angel is abundantly clear, repeating to Nephi multiple times what characterizes this church: it worships wealth and it oppresses the saints of God. The language in v. 5 is powerful: "[The church] slayeth the saints of God, yea, and tortureth them and bindeth them down, and yoketh them with a yoke of iron, and bringeth them down into captivity." There is no reason to think that these things are meant only metaphorically. These are actual events that have happened throughout human history when people have worshipped wealth. Colonialism, slavery, and war have all been, at their root, about commodifying people for the purpose of amassing riches. These forces have been some of the main drivers of human behavior throughout history. Today, we see them in punitive immigration policies, human trafficking, mass incarceration, sweatshops producing cheap goods, and laws and policies that punish the poor.

The values of the great and abominable church need to be eradicated from our society. But to do so, we need to look at our own organizations and institutions and our own history and see where we have worshipped at the altar of the great and abominable church. If we read these verses as if that evil church is always somewhere else and never within our midst, then we are missing what God is asking us to do. We have to remove it from our own walls and from our own hearts.

In a scriptural sense, the word "great" means enormous and powerful, not necessarily good. Just as God touches every life whether God is acknowledged or not, the great and abominable church also touches every life. It is also in the structures of the world, whether we see it there or not. The first thing we have to do is recognize and acknowledge it. See the marginalization, oppression, and suffering of others at the hands of a system that worships wealth. Don't miss the greatness of the abominable church by denying how pervasive it is. Its ability to move individuals and societies without us even knowing or seeing that it exists is part of what makes this church great. If we are under the delusion that the great and abominable church has not infiltrated our ranks and our mindsets, then we are missing its greatness. If we are not intentional in seeing it, we most certainly will miss it. There's a reason the angel has to tell Nephi to look. There's a reason the verses about worshipping wealth are done twice over (v. 7–8). To think that it's something outside of our churches, outside of our communities, outside of ourselves, makes it nearly impossible to eradicate. If we do not stand up and call it for what it is, we are complicit. We all need to ask ourselves, as the angel asked Nephi, "What beholdest thou?" All of us in religious communities need to answer that. What do we see? Who do we see? How are we complicit? Who in our midst is being bound, enslaved, and tortured? Part of our spiritual discipline should be to ask ourselves regularly those types of searching questions and hold ourselves accountable for the answers.

1 Nephi 13:12–18; 40–42

These verses have repeatedly been offered as a divine sanction of Christopher Columbus and as proof that white people hold the birthright to the Americas. This is troubling. Columbus, whose misguided navigation landed him in the Americas, would commit many atrocities in the name of exploration and that impact can still be witnessed today. Generally, European settlers treated Native Americans as sub-human, engaging in extraordinary levels of violence and deceit for generations.[26] It is hard to understand how Nephi could have seen a vision of European settlement and the genocide of Indigenous peoples and felt like it was sanctioned by God. Further complicating these verses is the fact that Nephi has *just seen* a vision of the great and abominable church and been told that successfully searching for wealth is not a sign of God's grace, yet Nephi writes, "And I beheld the Spirit of the Lord, that it was upon the Gentiles, and they did

---

26. Howard Zinn, *A People's History of the United States*, (New York: Harper Perennial, 2003), 25–26.

prosper and obtain the land for their inheritance." What do we make of this?

Understanding that Nephi is still raging, still grieving about the future destruction of his people, helps us to interpret the text. He is likely also in sensory overload at this point, having gone through a crash course on God's word and the history of the world.

A glimpse of Nephi's mental state is revealed in just how intensely Nephi attaches to the Gentiles. He fully adopts them as his own people, turning away from his blood kin, the Lamanites. He writes the Gentiles "obtain the land for their inheritance"—a land that only a little while ago was the inheritance of the descendants of Lehi—and that the Gentiles "were white, and exceedingly fair and beautiful, *like unto my people before they were slain.*" [emphasis added] "Like unto my people before they were slain" indicates that he has fully broken off blood ties and mentally bestowed his legacy on the Gentiles, creating a lineal connection between "his" people and the Gentiles that is not nearly as strong as the blood ties he has with his brothers. Furthermore, Nephi builds his part of connection with the Gentiles on phenotype, or the look of whiteness, which he deems aesthetically "fair and beautiful." While there are numerous problems with Nephi's claims, a few key issues must be addressed, especially when taking into account the social construction of race in the United States. First, not all Gentiles have white skin. Second, attaching beauty to skin color is a social ill that has been arguably a social ill that can be traced back to a misuse of scripture and corrupt cultural ideologies. Devastatingly, these ideas of surrounding whiteness as beautiful and righteous have been a historical and present-day source of so much harm and violence perpetrated on brown and black people in the world. In this vein, scripture and our rationalization of this type of text is complicit in the pain and devastation that has been exacted throughout the generations.

Unable to obtain justice against his brothers in this life, Nephi may see justice in a distant future and a distant people. In his eyes, those actions naturally must come from God. Of course the Gentiles have divine right. Justice is finally being served. Nephi's anger and heartbreak lead him to see the world in an extremely bifurcated way: he sees nothing good from his brothers' descendants and aggrandizes the work of Gentiles and more than that, he places God with them and on their side. It is good versus evil, and for Nephi, good is finally going to win. He is forming theology at one of his darkest, most painful times.

The structure of this vision is crucial for our understanding. The angel warned Nephi about prosperity gospel through the vision of the great and abominable church, but in his grief, Nephi misses it.[27] We can't miss it. We have the gift of being emotionally removed and having the space to reread and ponder these verses. Our challenge is to take this slowly and not just lazily accept Nephi's interpretation. Sink into these words. Challenge them.

Another clue to us that Nephi may have skewed some of this vision comes from the last verses of this chapter. In what sounds like a gentle reminder to Nephi, the angel speaks of a universal, loving, and inclusive God. "[F]or there is one God and one Shepherd over all the earth. And the time cometh that he shall manifest himself unto all nations, both unto the Jews and also unto the Gentiles . . . and the last shall be first, and the first shall be last." This is a warning of how to read this text. Do not think that the Gentiles prospering and obtaining land is a sign of God's preference. The angel says that the last shall be first and the first shall be last. The angel tells him that there is one Shepherd over all the earth.

1 Nephi 14:15–20

The phrase "wars and rumors of wars" appears nine times in scripture, seven of which occur in books that Joseph Smith translated or revealed. It is usually used to describe the final, most terrible time

---

[27]. "Put simply, the prosperity gospel is the belief that God grants health and wealth to those with the right kind of faith." Kate Bowler. "Death, the Prosperity Gospel, and Me" *New York Times*, Feb. 13, 2016.

before the Second Coming of Christ. Why is the rumor of war so awful as to be included? Obviously, war itself is destructive and heartbreaking. Is just the threat of war so bad as to warrant its use in the description of the worst of times?

The Book of Mormon seems to boldly answer in the affirmative. The absence of war does not mean there's peace. But having rumors of wars, even without the actual outbreak of war, creates a constant sense of threat and looming adversarial sentiments.

To achieve real growth, societies require the work of positive peace—a peace in which they are creating structures to ensure peace, justice, equality, and safety. The Reverend Dr. Martin Luther King Jr. criticized those who seek to uphold a negative peace, an order without justice.[28] The theme of peace and war is one of the most important of the Book of Mormon. While there are brief stretches of positive peace, such as the time after Christ's visit, when there is no tribalism and "no poor among them," there are many times of war and rumors of war. A mere ceasefire, a time when the Lamanites and Nephites are not actively killing one another, does not necessarily suggest that a positive peace is at work within community. The message is that a negative peace is an absence of justice. To avoid violence in its various forms, including structural violence, we need to be building towards a positive peace, a peace where justice exists.

The phrase "mother of abominations" and "mother of harlots" is worth examining, if for no other reason than the harsh language surrounding "mother" is somewhat uncommon in scripture. In this

---

28. "I had hoped that the white moderate would understand that the present tension in the South is a necessary phase of the transition from an obnoxious negative peace, in which the Negro passively accepted his unjust plight, to a substantive and positive peace, in which all men will respect the dignity and worth of human personality. Actually, we who engage in nonviolent direct action are not the creators of tension. We merely bring to the surface the hidden tension that is already alive. We bring it out in the open, where it can be seen and dealt with." Martin Luther King, Jr. *Letter from Birmingham Jail*. Martin Luther King Center for Nonviolent Social Change, 1968.

case, invoking "mother" implies creation and birth. The abomination is created, it does not exist ex nihilo. Thus, abomination did not happen without willing participants.

The word harlot needs to be reclaimed in scripture. The word has strong culturally derived, sexist connotations as it is typically only used to condemn women. The word is most useful when we can strip it of its gendered meaning. In these verses, "harlot" should be more broadly defined to describe indiscriminate and careless acts of creation. This understanding removes the damaging gendered connotation and reveals how people have acted with both intention and heedlessness. The reality of that seeming contradiction can be seen in the way perpetrators of war and terrorism use violence as both a means and an end.

It is in the midst of this abominable creation that God's work starts. God comes in response to the creation of abominations, not despite it. This should give humans hope. One reason for Christ's arrival into the world is to dispel darkness and offer relief. The abominable church has led directly to war and structural violence.

1 Nephi 14:19-26

Finally, Nephi writes about seeing the apostle John making a record of Christ. The commencement of the Father's work through the entrance of Christ in a dark moment of unholiness is beautiful. This is immediately followed with the arrival of the twelve apostles, which is complex. Along with seeing John in white, making a record of the Messiah, Nephi would have seen Judas. Nephi may or may not have understood what Judas would do, but his presence underlines the human imperfection that surrounds Christ's perfection.

The vision closes with the prophet and recorder (Nephi) watching an ancestral prophet (John) record. The message is clear: those who learn of Christ need to testify of Christ through writing their own stories and experiences. Ultimately, this is God's great plan for fighting the great and abominable church: send Christ, then let people make a record of it. But just as there is a clear instruction that the work of Christ is carried out by those who testify of Jesus, there is also a caveat: not all truth should be shared. Nephi closes by stating that God has limited what he is allowed to write. The truth is holy, but it requires gentle handling. There's a dual responsibility in knowing the words and works of God: to share and to hold back. Be a person who God can trust with both.

This incredible vision reaches soaring heights of hope and plunges into the depths of despair, rises up and then sinks back down. Nephi sees the tree of life, the birth of Christ, the destruction of his people, and the creation of the great and abominable church as a response to his inquiry about Lehi's vision. Emotionally intense, with all the grief, rage, grace and joy of a lifetime boiled down to three chapters of scripture, Nephi receives far more than he requested.

Throughout Nephi's questioning journey, we find that at certain times answers are swift and expansive, and at other times they are seemingly slow in coming or not a direct response to his original question. Nephi does such a wonderful job of showing us the spectrum of God's responses to our inquiries. Answers may come in visions and visitations. Some questions result in opportunities to practice patience and persistence. And sometimes it seems that God is not inclined to offer the full scope of the divine plan. One thing is certain in Nephi's story—God does answer.

1 Nephi 15:5

The overriding emotion Nephi feels as he returns to his family is grief. His sorrow is so intense that he believes that his "afflictions were great above all." Nephi is in an emotional place of believing that he is the most persecuted person on earth. He is not alone in this feeling. Many people, including prophets, have felt the same way.[29]

---

29. Numbers 11:15, I Kings 19:7–18

But it's worth considering, as we did in 1 Nephi 12:22–23, that the ideas that come out of Nephi when he is in that much pain may not be absent of his hurt. Nephi's pain is all consuming at this point and he needs space to grieve. We, the readers of the text, can give him that by weighing his words with the sentiment from whence they are derived.

How does Nephi's emotional state affect how he interacts with his brothers? He doesn't extend much compassion or love. He wields truth, but not in a kind way. His words lack compassion or care for the fraternal relationship. And while just a few chapters earlier the family was able to hold Sariah in her grief and doubt, what emerges in this moment of sorrow is additional conflict. Perhaps this is because Laman and Lemuel are too hardened against Nephi to reach out to him. Perhaps it is because Nephi cannot or will not share why he grieves. But it's sad to watch here as Nephi presents a didactic call to repentance without opening up a space for real connection or healing.

1 Nephi 16:1–2

When Laman and Lemuel cry out that "Thou hast declared unto us hard things, more than we are able to bear," Nephi responds that "the guilty taketh the truth to be hard, for it cutteth them to the very center." Nephi hasn't said anything that particularly condemns Laman and Lemuel or singles them out for their behavior. He has spoken in generalities: explaining the symbolism of Lehi's dream and teaching of a final judgment. That Laman and Lemuel see themselves in Nephi's words and are upset by them is a sign of at least some openness to the Spirit. It is when we go into a space of reckoning and emerge feeling content with ourselves that we ought to be worried. Being called to repentance, looking at the beam in our own eye, and seeing our own brokenness is hard work. For those who are doing that work, it will often feel harder than we can bear. It will feel like we are being cut to our center. That's how we know that it can be transformational, if we allow the discomfort to move us into healing. Hebrews 12:6 tells us that God chastens those whom God loves. If we are too hardened to be cut to our center, then we cannot experience the healing of Christ.

1 Nephi 16:18–39

Two stories take place back to back in Nephi's narrative concerning people complaining to God about their circumstances in the wilderness. In the first, the family's hunting bows breaking leaves them without a way to get food. In the second, Ishmael dies and his daughters cry out in grief. In both, Nephi emerges as the hero for trusting God and not murmuring. Is his condemnation of his family fair? Was God truly angry at the complaints? Nephi's narrative firmly answers both of these questions in the affirmative. It is worth pondering whether Nephi's understanding of the nature of God is correct or complete.

In the first case, all of the hunting bows in the family have broken. We don't know how long they have gone without food, but the family is hungry. Nephi writes that they are "suffering" and "sorrowful." This indicates that they have been hungry for a while and that they believe they will die in the wilderness. In the second case, Ishamel dies, apparently prematurely and from the harsh conditions of their lives. In addition to their grief, his daughters believe that they will also die. They are struggling with "hunger, thirst, and fatigue."

Are anger, fear, and frustration unacceptable to God? Writers of scripture from the Psalmist to Joseph Smith have cried out in their darkest moments. God did not answer them with condemnation. In Nephi's narrative, God actually withholds food from the family until they repent of their murmuring. This is a level of manipulation and punishment that seems incongruent with divinity. If we have to tailor our relationship with God, if we have to censor our communication, if God can't take all of the human experience, then it's hard to say who God is. There are likely times in all of our lives when we are so filled with despair, so hopeless in the face of loss, that we cry out against the heavens and asked, "Where are you, God?" It is hard to believe God would condemn us in those times. Life is unfair and it breaks heavier on certain people. How can we worship a God who doesn't allow us to be upset with that? This text is not allowing for the expansiveness of what it is to live a human life and walk alongside God.

With these stories, it's important to recognize the context of Nephi's life. Nephi is living in the time of Jeremiah. He has seen a vision of Christ, but his theology has grown up in a pre-Christian era. He is, essentially, an Old Testament prophet. The God of the Old Testament is, at times, unbending and impersonal, a God who takes sides and destroys and seeks vengeance. Nephi interprets his spiritual experiences through the lens of his culture, so it is unsurprising that Nephi's God seems to lack compassion and forgiveness. Nephi is a Law of Moses prophet and it shows, from the way he casually excludes the women in the narrative to his inclination to condemn people for their failings. If Nephi's text were included in the Old Testament, which is where it belongs in the historical narrative, Mormon readers would allow for a changed understanding of God. We would read Nephi with the knowledge that a new, higher law would come forward with Christ, and that law would bring us into personal relationship with a gentler God.

1 Nephi 17: 1–3; 20

The first few verses of chapter 17 speak to the brutality of refugee life. Any time a group of people move from one land to another with uncertainty and danger, women will bear the brunt of that affliction with their bodies. They will bring forth life in the midst of turmoil and hardship. The refugee experience is exponentially harder for women because of what their bodies go through. They have to travel the same distance, eat the same food, sleep in the same harsh conditions, and do it through menstruation, pregnancy, nursing, and childcare.

Nephi writes in verse 2 that the women were strong like unto the men. Nephi is, at least, recognizing a portion of what the women have gone through. But he also misses something fundamental because he uses a patriarchal lens that sees male strength as the highest standard. If the women are doing the work of men and the work of women, then they are actually stronger than the men. These women are traveling through the wilderness just as the men are, but they're doing it while also doing the labor that comes with being female. They've been giving life, nursing babies, and carrying children on their backs. They're not *as strong as* men, they're *stronger* than men. Nephi misses this because of his cultural background, but modern-day readers can do better and recognize the work of women who carve out life in circumstances that deal in death.

On some level, Laman and Lemuel seem to understand that concept better than Nephi. They appear to show more empathy for what their wives have suffered. Nephi and his brothers describe the experiences of the women in very different ways. For Nephi, God nourished and strengthened the women, "provid[ing] means whereby they [could] accomplish the thing which he has commanded them" (v. 3). Laman and Lemuel, living and witnessing the same events, say that the women would have been better to have died in Jerusalem rather than undergoing the suffering they experienced in the wilderness (v. 20). The juxtaposition of these two versions of the same story shows the importance of personal narrative. Laman and Lemuel see unimaginable hardship. Nephi sees God endlessly blessing them. The person who tells the story has the power to define the meaning of that story.

If indeed the storyteller has that much influence, then we should have the women's voices here. The brothers give alternative perspectives about the female experience, but we still have not heard from the women. Their experiences were arguably just as diverse as their husbands'—some of them may have wished they had died in Jerusalem and some may have felt God moving in their lives. It's not that the men's narrative is necessarily incorrect; it's that without hearing directly from the women, we don't truly know. This is a moment when hearing directly from them would be an enormous benefit to the reader. We need to hear from more than just their male counterparts. It would be extraordinary here to have a firsthand account of even one of these women who gave birth in the wilderness while eating raw meat. The only thing that all the men can agree on is that the women went through terrible hardships. There is something in the women's silent suffering that we need to recognize.

In this way, scriptural text fails us as a Christian community. It fails us when the women of the holy text do not get to tell their stories and share their journeys with God. At best this is a slight to these women and at worst it is a grave injustice. Their stories could have informed and inspired our own journeys as students of the Book of Mormon and followers of Christ. We get to mourn that we only hear about them through the lens of their brothers, husbands and sons. For their words could have informed and taught us so much of the wilderness experience and a faith that endures. Their stories matter.

1 Nephi 17:19

We see a different kind of cruelty here from Laman and Lemuel. They are delighting in someone else's failure. They are happy to see him feel small and helpless. This is another step in the progression of abuse in this story. Even with how terrible the previous physical violence was, it was impulsive and done under extreme stress. The belittling here is calculated to inflict harm. It's difficult to imagine the harm done by someone close to you looking for you to fail with God. There are moments in our lives when we want people to know that we've heard God's voice. We want our lives to work smoothly because we want others to see that we have God with us. But God doesn't always show up in that way. Sometimes we will fall on our faces even when we're following God. Some people, like Laman and

Lemuel, relish watching others fail in their efforts. That delight in failure can prompt people to question their own inspiration or doubt their relationship with God. This form of spiritual abuse is one of the cruelest acts someone can commit against another person.

1 Nephi 17:45–47

The idea of being past feeling is an important one. There is a spiritual space that is possible to reach only when a person has gone counter to God for so long that God cannot move within that person anymore. This is a damnation moment. Nephi is describing the loss of the Divine as a loss of feeling. At the beginning of chapter 16, Laman and Lemuel say that Nephi has declared a hard thing to them, words that are harder than they can bear. At that point, they are not past feeling. By chapter 17, they have worked up to the point where they couldn't feel the Divine anymore, through the upscaling of violence to emotional abuse to attempted patricide (v. 44). Somewhere on that journey of harming those around them they have lost the ability to feel. Feeling is how we maintain our connection to humanity and the Divine. Laman and Lemuel's disregard for humanity has withered their connection to God.

Nephi's description illuminates further understanding when he writes that Laman and Lemuel couldn't feel the words of God. He doesn't write that they couldn't hear them or understand them—in fact, Nephi writes that Laman and Lemuel *have* heard the words of God. But they did not feel them. It is the feeling experience that draws us to God. What does it look like to hear the word of God but be past feeling? It is to hear the cries stemming from the injustice of the world and not share in that anguish. Such anguish should catalyze us to move in ways to relieve the suffering. The condition of being "past feeling' is a degradation of the Light of Christ we are born with, a hardening of one's own humanity, and inevitably results in our inability to truly see one another.

In direct contrast to Laman and Lemuel, Nephi is full of feeling. He is so overcome with feeling that his "soul is rent with anguish" and his "heart is pained." He physically loses strength from his emotional grief. A call to the prophetic is a walk in grief. Those who teach truth and walk with people in their iniquity must deal in deep sadness. Far from being past feeling, disciples take on the heartbreak of the world, feeling it deeply within themselves. If the absence of the Divine is apathy—being past feeling—than the presence of the Divine is to feel.

1 Nephi 17:50–51

We have to admire Nephi's optimism and his trust in God. Nephi builds his relationship with God in knowing the stories of the past. He knows that God has fulfilled promises in the past. He calls on the past to give him this profound trust in the future. If God came through before, God will come through for me now. Nephi is an example of seeing how God showed up in the past in the stories of our forefathers and foremothers and using that to be able to show up for the work of today. This is one of the strengths and powers to knowing one's own spiritual and ancestral history.

1 Nephi 18:1–2

If a person is creating something holy that has never been done before, don't be surprised if it requires curious workmanship. Anything that will take people to new lands will rarely be in the manner of men. Other people are going to look at it and think that it's absurd. Nephi repeats again and again that his ship is not anything that humans would have thought up. In ministry, many of the things we do will not be in the manner of men.

1 Nephi 18:11–16

This is one of the most harrowing stories in this family's journey. Nephi is bound and beat up by his older brothers. He gives us, the reader, a detailed description of this episode of abuse.

The details of the violence are symbolically destructive to the soul. As if Nephi being bound for days is not bad enough, the fact is that he is bound on his ship, a thing he created in partnership with God, and bound with cords that he most likely placed on that ship. To have those things he has built and prepared in faith and hope be later weaponized against him seems particularly cruel.[30]

1 Nephi 19:1

Nephi states here the exact parameters of his record: it is of "my father, and also our journeyings in the wilderness, and the prophecies of my father; and also many of mine own prophecies." Although Nephi states that he is making a record of "our" journeys, there is only his voice and his narrative. He is speaking on behalf of a larger community. There are many versions of the family's journeyings that would also be true and valid, but we don't get those. We have to remember that history and scripture filter through the lens of the person telling the story. Not everyone in this group would tell their story in the same way. That doesn't mean that what Nephi writes is wrong, it just means that we need to be careful with it because it's easy to assume that the one story is the only story.

Most scripture follows in that same pattern: there is one voice to tell the narrative. The Gospels provide an important exception: Matthew, Mark, Luke, and John each tell their own version of the

---

30. It is worth considering how we take what other people have created with God and turn it around to hurt them. Churches have at times done this with LGBTQ people who have done missionary work, sung in the choir, taught children, and done other work to build the community. That same community then turns around and preaches limits on God's love and harms the people who helped build the church. This weaponizes people's own work against them.

life of Christ. Christians have struggled for years with the discrepancies among these accounts. In the Gospels, four different lenses were given and, predictably, they tell similar but different stories. We are left to grapple with the complexity that results. That's a good thing. A single narrative narrows the story to a monolithic view.

The Book of Mormon has just one narrator for every story. Again, that doesn't make that narration wrong, but readers ought to be aware of the voices that are not shared. The most obvious example is the absence of any female narrative. These characters are not unimportant, just unheard. Readers should carefully consider who is in the room but silent because of the limited narrative that we have. Nephi specifically says here that he is choosing to concentrate on the record of his father, their journeyings in the wilderness, the prophecies of his father, and his own prophecies. Full stop. It is all about him and Lehi. We don't know if other people were asked to contribute a few lines, but we do know that we don't get anything from anyone else and that Nephi explicitly is interested only in those narrow parameters.

1 Nephi 19:3

Nephi writes that he is making a record of "the ministry and the prophecies." Latter-day Saints don't often talk about how ministry and prophecy work together. Part of prophecy is divine knowledge, speaking into the current time about what God wants the people to do. Ministry is about carrying that out. Prophecy and ministry are not meant to be divorced from one another, but in fact, they work together in tandem. When we have the prophetic without ministry, prophets are left weeping and wailing because they are crying out against evil but no one does anything about it. When ministry is without prophecy, it is anemic and directionless, losing its purpose and energy before work can be done.

Matthew 25 describes feeding the hungry, clothing the naked, welcoming the stranger, and visiting the sick and incarcerated. In addition to that valuable work, ministry includes recognizing how certain historical and current economic policies make life harder for the poor.[31] It is also the work of asking for a society where no one has to go without access to healthcare.[32] Ministry is also the work of fighting against policies, practices and laws that target and disproportionately incarcerate black and brown people.[33] It is the work of immigration and how our country welcomes the strangers.[34] Yes, prophecy should and does help us, as Christians, envision the myriad of ways of moving in ministry. While it is crucial to see to the physical needs of one another, there is also a profound call for us, as believers, to do the work to upset systems, laws and policies that continue to harm and oppress.

The other phrase to note in this verse is "also for other wise purposes, which purposes are known unto the Lord." Nephi's faith journey is not an easy one. Although he's sometimes privileged to receive incredible visions and direction, he's also often not given answers for why or how he should do something. At times he is doing things one way and has to stop and do it another way. Or he's commanded to do something painstaking and laborious, such as create two sets of records, without an explanation for why. In such times, we have to simply believe that the Lord has a wise purpose. We have no indication that Nephi ever got an explanation for why he ought to keep these two separate records. Given that he is writing later in his life, it's fair to assume that he was never told. It could have

---

31. Joseph E. Stiglitz. *The Price of Inequality: How Today's Divided Society Endangers Our Future.* New York: W.W. Norton & Company, 2013.
Mehrsa Baradaran. *How the Other Half Banks: Exclusion, Exploitation, and the Threat to Democracy.* Cambridge: Harvard University Press: 2015.
32. Jacob Bor, Gregor H Cohen, Sandro Galea. "Population Health in an Era of Rising Income Inequality: USA 1980–2015." *The Lancet 389*, 10077 (April 8, 2017): 1475.
33. Michelle Alexander. *The New Jim Crow: Mass Incarceration in the Age of Color Blindness.* New York: The New Press, 2010.
34. Karen Gonzalez, *The God Who Sees: Immigrants, the Bible and the Journey to Belong.* Harrisburg, Virginia: Herald Press, 2019.

been a lifelong work that he did, without ever knowing why. We may never know our full impact or why we undertook the work that we did. In this way, faith is the unknowing. It's the unknowing walk into the unknown while believing in a wise purpose. This type of trusting walk with God requires sensitivity to the Spirit. It also takes bravery to follow your divine promptings, perhaps never knowing, the extent of the purpose.

1 Nephi 19:6

One of the extraordinary characteristics of writers of the Book of Mormon is their ready admission of their flaws. Nephi does this in two ways here: first, by noting that he may not have gotten everything right in his record and that there may be mistakes. Secondly, by using the language "I think it [to] be sacred" instead of "it is sacred." He is admitting that his judgment may be wrong but that he's doing his best work. That kind of humility is inspiring and sets an example for us to follow. Even those who are closest to God readily acknowledge their capacity to err.

1 Nephi 19:9

The language describing Jesus in the Book of Mormon is breathtaking. The Jesus of the Book of Mormon is the most compassionate version in all of scripture. Book of Mormon prophets see Him as overflowing with loving kindness, long suffering, and compassion. The words they use are poetry. Even at the same time in history as some Old Testament prophets, the exilic people of North and South America paint a very different picture of the Messiah. Readers of the Book of Mormon should pay close attention to the kind of words used to describe Jesus. One way the Book of Mormon reveals its importance in the scriptural canon is in its continual and expanding verbiage describing the loving and compassionate nature of Jesus.

1 Nephi 19:20

Nephi has intense physical reactions to spiritual experiences. At times he is made impossibly strong and another time he is filled with an electrical current. Here, he is so drained from the "workings of the spirit" that he is wearied until his "joints are weak." Anyone who is going through the prophetic experience will pay a toll for observing evil, watching destruction, and doing the work of God. Knowing the worst of what exists in the world does not allow a person to come out unscathed. Prophets are not exempt from calamities. Nephi is telling us that there is a physical price he pays for living into God's commands and seeing what he sees in the world. Nephi shows us that spiritual work comes with a physical price.

1 Nephi 19:23

In order for scriptures to be for our profit and learning, we have to liken *all* scriptures to ourselves. At times, there is a tendency to see or align ourselves with those that we see as the good people in scripture. We would rather see how we are like Nephi than see how we are like Laman and Lemuel. But if we are going to engage in real work with scripture, we have to see ourselves in all the parts. Scriptures have the ability to show us the full spectrum of our strengths and weaknesses, but only if we allow them. We have to be willing to see ourselves denying Jesus three times as well as seeing ourselves leaving our nets and following Jesus. We can see ourselves as a female witness to Resurrection whom nobody believes as well as one of the men who ignore those good women. That's how we can gain perspective and see our own failings and brokenness as well as our beauty and faith. Liken all scriptures unto yourself, not just the parts you want affirmed, but also the parts of you that you have never faced, the parts that are dark and buried. That's what scripture should bring out, so that we can start correcting and learning. If you want to profit and learn from scripture, don't make it an anemic study. If we allow them, the scriptures have the capacity to transform us.

1 Nephi 22:6-14, 25

Nephi's explanation of the relationship between the Lamanites and the Gentiles is convoluted. First, Nephi tells his brothers that their descendants will be nursed by the Gentiles. There is beautiful language of growth and development as they are nursed, then carried in arms, then carried on shoulders. This is language of a people helping other people, community helping other communities in their walk with God.

But then in the following verse, the Gentiles are a mighty nation that scatter the descendants of Lehi's sons. There is a sharp reversal, as the Gentiles appear to become the enemies of the House of Israel in verse 7, then change again to do a marvelous work that will benefit Israel in verse 8. Nephi describes a turbulent relationship that at times is beautiful and cooperative and other times is violent and ugly. This complexity breaks down the idea of tribalism, as it is unclear who are allies and who are enemies. In verses 13-14 this becomes even more complicated, as people turn against their own kind and war seems to blanket the earth. All of this confusion seems deliberate, as if mixing up all the tribes and -ites into one big messy pot is a lesson to teach Laman and Lemuel that those labels and groups don't matter. In the end, none of the manmade divisions among the people will matter because the only important thing will be those who follow God and those who don't. Nephi is almost underlining to his brothers: just try to follow who is with us and who is against us. You won't be able to. And it doesn't matter.

This will play out in a similar way in the rest of the Book of Mormon, as the Nephites and Lamanites fight against each other, then come together peacefully, then separate again, then unite with other groups, then switch places, then finally descend so deeply into violence that their divisions become meaningless. In the end, the only naming that will matter is the answer to God's question in Matthew 25:40: "What have you done unto the least of these?" What will matter is who knew and served God. Nephi tells his brothers, in verse 25,

"And there shall be one fold and one shepherd; and he shall feed his sheep, and in him they shall find pasture." The old tribes and labels will fall away and we will be of one fold with God as our Shepherd.

1 Nephi 22:31

Nephi opened his account by emphasizing that this was his narrative ("I, Nephi") and has repeated that throughout this book. Interestingly, he ends his book by reminding readers that other voices are out there. While focusing only on his own story, he finishes by encouraging readers to seek out and give credence to others' testimonies.

2 NEPHI

2 Nephi 1:6

At first reading, this verse may seem confusing. "None come into this land save they shall be brought by the hand of the Lord," doesn't seem true when so many people came to the Americas against their will. Is Nephi implying that slaves were brought by the hand of the Lord?

Here, including the cross-reference is vital. In 2 Nephi 10: 22, Lehi writes, "the Lord God has led away from time to time from the house of Israel, according to his will and pleasure. And now behold, the Lord remembereth all them who have been broken off, wherefore he remembereth us also." The ancestors of everyone in the Americas fall into four categories: they are either Native Americans, immigrants, refugees, or enslaved people. All of those four categories have experienced violence in some form. But the cross-reference tells us that no one is forgotten, no matter how they arrived and how they were broken. America is a land of the broken-offs. God keeps an eye on those who are broken off. So perhaps we can read 2 Nephi 1:6 as "There shall none come into this land save they shall be remembered by the Lord."

2 Nephi 1:7–11

The theology that Lehi espouses in these verses is troubling. The language he uses about "possessing" the land and his repeated claim that obedience to the commandments will guarantee safety and prosperity are problematic. The biggest issue is his belief that obedience guarantees security. "If it so be that they shall keep his commandments they shall be blessed upon the face of this land, and there shall be none to molest them, nor to take away the land of their inheritance; and they shall dwell safely forever." Given Lehi's life experiences, the idea that he is claiming that obedience to the commandments guarantees safety is almost jaw-dropping. It was, after all, his own obedience to God that caused him to lose his home and wealth in Jerusalem and spend years on the point of starvation in the wilderness. He has witnessed, and repeatedly invokes in the following chapters, the suffering of his family members that has followed their commitment to their faith. His own family's experience belies the claims about God that he is making in these verses.

Using scriptural imagination, we can approach these verses in different ways. The first is to see Lehi as prophesying from the point of privilege, a somewhat surprising position, given his years spent suffering in the wilderness. But Lehi has also lived the life of a wealthy elite in Jerusalem. His words here sound more like he is looking through the lens of that life. Lehi's privileged life in Jerusalem never fully left him, which means that his theology is affected by it. It's hard to condemn him for viewing the world through the status he enjoyed in Jerusalem for so much of his life. But we have to remember, as readers, that his words stem from his background and that at this moment, he's not moving in his own experiences of loss, poverty and hunger. Given the limited record we have of Lehi's words, it is tragic that in this moment he teaches a theology of prosperity gospel and a vending-machine God. It would be so valuable to hear about how Lehi viewed God in the wilderness, when he was struggling to survive on raw meat and keep his family from disintegration. Lehi doesn't speak to those experiences. He doesn't answer the question of what "blessed" looks like when all the material wealth has been stripped away.

The second perspective is to recognize that Lehi's time as a refugee affected his theology. Lehi doesn't seem to be saying that prospering involves having vast riches; for him, prosperity appears to be about safety and security—a defensive posture of merely being left alone, having a place of refuge, a space and time in which he and his descendants can live without fear. Given Lehi's life experiences, safety is interwoven with exclusivity: his people can only live in safety if the land belongs only to them. He has felt too many threats, many from his own neighbors and even family members, to believe that peace is otherwise possible. Readers can strive to empathize with the fear and sadness that caused this kind of desire, even if the theology it provokes is not on a good foundation.

Lehi's language about the land as an inheritance is also troubling. Inheritance implies ownership. Lehi has only recently arrived in the Americas, a land where there are already other people living. Lehi repeatedly writes of "possessing" the land, which is very different from a mindset of caretaking and stewardship. Lehi seems to be claiming an entitlement to the land, instead of acknowledging that the land and all its wealth belongs to God. While the choice of language may seem small, it affects a theological mindset about land and people that warps the understanding of God's blessings.

We can't silently pass by Lehi's words here, because not naming it corrupts our own theology. We have to push back against Lehi here and ask ourselves why he is making these claims about God. Lehi lived most of his life with power and wealth and then spent the end of his life in suffering and destitution. That will affect how he speaks. We can simultaneously feel empathy for Lehi and let his words warn us of the blinders that we can put up when we have lived in privilege. In the narrative of Lehi's family, God has shown up in loss of land, in wilderness, in wandering, and in hunger. Obedience has been no guarantee of security and wealth. Don't let Lehi's words confuse that.

2 Nephi 2:1

In chapters 2–3, Lehi is specifically speaking to his sons born in the wilderness. That's significant, particularly since Lehi repeats himself again and again, calling Jacob his "first-born in the wilderness" and Joseph his "last-born in the wilderness." These two children are almost from a different family, having never experienced a privileged life in Jerusalem that their elder brothers and parents had. They were born into refugee life. The result is an interesting perspective. Lehi's message to them offers a deeper theology than he gave in any other account.

"Thou art my firstborn in the wilderness"—Lehi doesn't step around the situation in which Jacob was born. It's hard to imagine what it does to a child to say, "You were born in the hardest time of my life" and to repeatedly connect a child's name to suffering. "And behold in thy childhood thou hast suffered afflictions and much sorrow, because of the rudeness of thy brethren." Jacob has suffered. He was born in affliction and much sorrow, but the suffering comes from his brothers. He shares Nephi's experience of being a victim of domestic abuse. So while Lehi makes it clear that the wilderness was a time of suffering, what comes to the top is not necessarily the hunger, exhaustion, and instability that resulted from their physical circumstances. The suffering Lehi names comes from family. Jacob was born into a highly violent situation, without even having to touch the experience of the wilderness. This is a child who has experienced deep trauma. This child is acquainted with grief.

2 Nephi 2:2–3

"Nevertheless." Readers should always note a "nevertheless" because it means that the speaker is about to introduce some kind of tension and paradox. It means that something is being inserted or injected that will push up against what was just said. It may be that there are two truths standing in opposition yet happening simultaneously. A "nevertheless" lets readers know that there is complexity, that in the midst of something that seems straightforward, something deeper is happening. Real lives are full of "nevertheless" complicating moments. We should not expect monochromatic simplicity.

In this case, Lehi's "nevertheless" is that in the midst of Jacob's terrible afflictions, God consecrated Jacob's suffering. The phrase that may be difficult to understand is "for thy gain." Can Lehi say to an abused person that his suffering is for his good? To consecrate something means to name it and give it up to God. If we turn over our afflictions, can gain mean a healing? What about faithful people who don't experience healing? These are difficult theological questions that Lehi raises with the statement that a person's suffering can be for their gain.

Lehi has watched the abuse and suffering of his children. At this point, turning over guilt and sorrow to God and praying for Jacob to find the good in his experiences may be the only thing Lehi can do. Sometimes parents simply have to ask for a lot of grace where they fall short. For whatever reason, Lehi didn't stop his sons from committing violence. In some way, he had to consecrate that and say, "I hope you find healing, Jacob." This seems to be confirmed in verse 3, where Lehi says that his greatest hope is that Jacob will dwell safely with Nephi. After all that has happened, Lehi's wish is that his younger sons can find safety together.

2 Nephi 2:4

This is a fascinating glimpse into Jacob's spiritual journey. Although we don't get a full account of it, Jacob has beheld the fullness of time and has been redeemed. Not only has he had some kind of vision similar to what Nephi experienced earlier, Jacob has also had an experience with Christ that has made clear that his salvation is sure. Jacob is a spiritual giant. He was born in the wilderness and suffered many afflictions, including abuse from his brothers, and yet he beheld Christ as a young man. There also seems to be a miraculous healing that occurred, as Lehi says, "thou art blessed even as they unto whom he shall minister in the flesh." These two verses are powerful as we're just getting to know these last two sons. Jacob may have suffered under much sorrow, but he is spiritually strong. Still a young man at the time of Lehi's death, Jacob does incredible theological work in the harshest circumstances. Do not underestimate the two born in the wilderness.

2 Nephi 2:6

The Savior is full of grace and truth. Grace and truth go together, and there is a deep theological loss when one is wielded without the other. If you are a truth-teller who does not extend grace, you will harm those around you whom you claim to be helping. To tell the truth does not exonerate a person from cruelty if that person has weaponized it by withholding grace.

On the other side, grace without truth is, as Dietrich Bonhoeffer wrote, a "cheap grace"—one that is unaware of what has been sacrificed on each person's behalf. Grace paired with truth reveals a true understanding of the gospel, what Bonhoeffer calls a "costly grace." He writes, "Such grace is costly because it calls us to follow, and it is grace because it calls us to follow Jesus Christ. It is costly because it costs a man his life, and it is grace because it gives a man the only true life. It is costly because it condemns sin, and grace because it justifies the sinner. Above all, it is costly because it cost God the life of his Son: 'ye were bought at a price,' and what has cost God much cannot be cheap for us. Above all, it is grace because God did not reckon his Son too dear a price to pay for our life, but delivered him up for us. Costly grace is the Incarnation of God."[1] Grace and truth must be kept in union.

---

1. Dietrich Bonhoeffer. *The Cost of Discipleship.* New York: Macmillan, 1959.

2 Nephi 2:7

The language of "a broken heart and a contrite spirit" can be hard to face. It means that to know God deeply is to have your heart broken. Although ancient writers may not have understood the physiological implications, the meaning for modern readers, with additional scientific knowledge, is even more informative. The heart is a muscle, so it's not something that breaks. Muscles are strained, they are swollen, they are torn, they even die. They do not break like a bone. And yet our hearts must break. And even after our hearts are broken—something that sounds like death to a body—we must keep going. This is something that only makes sense to God.

Walking with God is a deeply breaking experience. Christ offered himself as a sacrifice for sin, breaking his own heart and offering a contrite spirit—*"Thy will be done"*—in the process. Christ suffered. We can expect that following this God will lead to times of deep grief. The requirements for moving in God's offered grace are a broken heart and contrite spirit.

2 Nephi 2:11

It's worth noting that Lehi once again invokes the phrase, "my firstborn in the wilderness" in conjunction with his claim that there is opposition in all things. For Lehi, the time in the wilderness marks the epitome of suffering and hardship in the path of following God. He seems to be continually trying to understand why his family had to go through that time.

Lehi's theology is problematic. From a certain perspective his claims make sense: it's difficult to appreciate sunshine without rain or food without hunger. And yet, to tell someone who has experienced a lifetime of abuse that righteousness could not come to pass without wickedness—essentially claiming that the spiritual encounters Jacob had with Christ would not have happened without suffering—is problematic. Trauma-induced theology, birthed out of deeply harmful, hurtful seasons, can be dangerous. That doesn't mean that it's wrong, it just means that we need to be particularly careful with it and hold space for the grief that accompanies it. When people are speaking out of a time in which they experienced deep affliction, putting those words in the context of the speaker's emotional state is critical. What they have experienced will shape their view of God. What Lehi says here is not bad theology, it's just the theology of his now. All of us are allowed to move in the theology of our now, communicating with the God we know in our now. But readers have the responsibility of placing those words in context. This means understanding that this is the theology of a man who is reflecting, as he dies, on a life of suffering and a son who has gone through deep trauma but who also has an amazing testimony of God. What does that intersection look like? For Lehi, at this time in his life, it looks like there is opposition in all things and that suffering is necessary.

It may help to remember that this is the theological place that Lehi has reached over many decades. While this is a more complex theology than we got in the previous chapter, it still eliminates much of the process of getting there. We're not invited into Lehi's internal dialogue of struggling to understand why suffering occurs in this life. We miss the middle section and are moved straight to the final scene.

2 Nephi 2:23–25

This is the foundation for the Mormon theology of Eve. These verses probably offer Eve the most redemptive light in Christianity. Rather than the classical portrayal of the wicked temptress, we see her here as a wise and thoughtful woman. The scripture here places Eve as a key part of the plan of salvation and as someone who used her heart and her brain to choose the better part. This better understanding of Eve is one of the most feminist pillars of Mormon doctrine.

And yet, Eve still gets written out of the narrative. When Lehi writes that "Adam fell that men might be" he completely misses the critical point of the story: that Adam and Eve fell together, that they progressed together. Although the largest doctrinal effect of these verses is an improved understanding of Eve's choice to partake, the text almost immediately moves her out of the picture and focuses entirely on Adam. So while we have this feminist reading that places Eve in a position of authority and wisdom that she doesn't receive anywhere else in Christianity, but then drops all references to her and gives only Adam a voice and a place. Doctrinally, these verses are some of the most important in the Book of Mormon. The redemption of Eve is a moment of textual brilliance. And then the author falls back into patriarchy. Readers can claim these moments of beauty and acknowledge them and name them and refuse to let them go even when asking: What happened to Eve? Why does her name fade from the text?

2 Nephi 2:27–30

If we're going to talk about people having choice and being free to choose, we should acknowledge that some people are a lot more free than others. If a person's choices are between going hungry and breaking the law, they don't really have much choice. It is impossible to deny that other people's choices affect the scope of our own freedom to choose. In a fallen world, sometimes the ability to have morals and live by them is a privilege. We need to reflect on how free we are to live into our moral structure and how that freedom is derived. Under what circumstances would that moral structure break down? Would I believe in upholding the law if I had to steal food for starving children? What about if I had to flee the country of my birth, cross an international border with a small child because I was not safe in my home? Sometimes living into our morality is a privilege. We need to be very careful when we believe we have the moral high ground or when we say, "That person has to face their consequences because they made that choice." Sometimes that will certainly be true, but we need to think about whether they truly had a choice.

2 Nephi 3:1

Lehi is nothing if not steady in his language about his time in the wilderness. Joseph was born in the days of Lehi's greatest sorrow. Readers can think about other stories of women in history who have given birth in the most horrific of circumstances. Sometimes, in those situations, even the birth of a healthy baby wrought with sorrow due to horrible circumstances. Women have even been known to kill their newborn babies because they had nothing to offer them but a life of abject misery. So it's possible that the birth of these children was a joy in the midst of sorrow and it's also possible that it just felt like more grief. Or both. Lehi doesn't tell us.

2 Nephi 3:12

Here Lehi gives us a clear list of what the Book of Mormon ought to do. If people are using this text for purposes that run contrary to this list, then they are going against the authors' intent. The Book of Mormon is meant to grow together with the Bible. It confounds false doctrines, it ends contentions, it establishes peace, and it brings people to a knowledge of the past and of God's covenants. Lehi tells readers how to incorporate the Book of Mormon into our lives and gives us a good measure to how we're utilizing this holy text.

The idea that the Book of Mormon should grow together with other scripture is critical. The Bible and the Book of Mormon are two sagas of two groups of people separated by an ocean. Considering how many people in great pain and suffering have been transported across that ocean, it's a lovely idea to say that scriptures on the two sides could grow together toward peace. Even scriptures need community. The Old Testament, New Testament, Pearl of Great Price, Koran, Torah, Book of Mormon, and all other scripture are meant to grow together to put down bad doctrine, establish peace, and increase knowledge. They are a community of scripture, created for the purpose of uniting us in a sense of the Divine.

In any family, some people may remember things differently or forget details altogether. Being able to share memories and retell stories together helps everyone get closer to the truth. One of the greatest strengths of scripture is the multitude of voices. The writers are all telling their stories of their journeys with God and they all sound a little different. That adds fullness, because we're not all going to experience the same thing in the same way. It binds us to our foremothers and forefathers, and invites us to closely examine our stories. Maybe if we share notes and tell our stories together, we will be more aware of the parts that were never true, but that crept into the story over time. We need each other in the memory work with God. Scripture does that for us and for other books of scripture. We need each other to find and remember truth. Scriptures need a community of scripture.

2 Nephi 3:13

The text here is a little confusing, but it seems to refer to the text of the Book of Mormon, meaning that even scriptural text may at times be weak, but still lead to strength. And when is that weakness made strong? "[W]hen my work shall commence among *all* my people" (emphasis added). All of us. The weaknesses of scripture are turned into strengths when everyone is included. That inclusion is going to require the human process of engaging with one another, with scripture, and with God. It will be flawed and unclear. We will have to ask hard questions: How do we do this? Whose names were forgotten? Who was never mentioned? Whose voices still need to be included? That is the work of holy text. We analyze, we immerse ourselves, we wrestle with it, we grow into the text. And then we can name the weaknesses of the text and be better. God will still show up in the weakness. God is still strong. The writers of the Book of Mormon have already told us many times that there are errors in the text and asked us to show some grace. What we have to do is come together and commence the work.

2 Nephi 3:19–20

There are cries from the dust. Are we listening to those cries? The text tells us that those who cry are faithful, simple, and weak. While all scripture is universal, it is also tied to a geographical place. The Book of Mormon is particular to the Americas, so it will speak to the American story. When we consider who is crying from the dust, we can think particularly about which voices on the American continents have been oppressed. Whose voices have been ground into the dust? How will God fulfill God's promise to make them strong?

2 Nephi 4:1

It is counterintuitive to us that Nephi describes Lehi's words about Joseph of Egypt as prophecy. Often we think about prophecy as being about the future, but Lehi is speaking about something that has already happened. In truth, prophecy can shed light on the past, present and the future.

2 Nephi 4:2–5

We finally have a record of women being in the room during this time. Despite what Nephi might think, this is important information for us. Since verse 2 quotes Lehi as prophesying about *all* his seed, that means that women were included in these blessings.

It's also interesting to note that Lehi gives a special audience to the children of Laman and Lemuel. We don't have a record of him doing that with his other grandchildren. While we can only speculate why Lehi would choose to do this, it's worth considering how difficult it would be to be the children of Laman and Lemuel. The brothers have repeatedly shown their propensity toward violence and their willingness to harm people weaker than themselves. While there is no record of their behavior toward their wives and children, we can at least be sure that those children saw their fathers do horrific things toward Lehi, Nephi, Sam, Jacob, and Joseph. They have been witnesses to and perhaps victims of abuse. So it's powerful that they get this moment of extra love from their grandfather.

2 Nephi 4:14

After Lehi dies, the remainder of this chapter contains Nephi's words of grief. What is even harder for Nephi is during this time of great loss he must also engage with his violent brothers.

Nephi writes that he was constrained to speak to Laman and Lemuel, which indicates that he did not want to speak to them but felt compelled. In this moment, Nephi may be feeling the imminent break-up of his family and no longer wants to even talk with his brothers. What it must have meant to still converse with his brothers in the midst of losing his father.

2 Nephi 4:15

Whatever is on the other plates, on these ones Nephi has borne his soul. His writing is remarkably personal—he does not say that he is writing the things of God; it's the writings of his own soul. Repeatedly through these chapters we have seen Nephi pondering, wrestling with theology even after he's had revelations and visions. We can believe him that he writes the things of the soul because we've already witnessed it.

Nephi is at a point of great grief and he will have to gather his courage in order to separate from his brothers. Yet first, he will name what brings him joy. The word "delight" almost seems like an extravagance in this moment. It's childlike, invoking an innocence that we could have assumed Nephi left behind a long time ago. Even though he is pondering everything that he has seen and heard, and we know that he has seen and heard a great deal of sorrow, his soul still delights in the things of God. That's a powerful testimony of a person who has been through hell yet still finds joy in the Lord.

2 Nephi 4:17

With this "nevertheless" moment, Nephi begins his lamentation. There is almost a rhythm or a cadence to it. Nephi starts by naming where he is, then describes how he falls short, then circles back to how he has trusted in God. The message for us is that we can be tempted and actually groan with grief for our shortcomings and sins, but *nevertheless* . . . In this case, nevertheless is a restorative word. I am human and often fall short, but nevertheless, I know in whom I have trusted. These are two statements that we may feel uncomfortable putting together: that someone may be groaning under sin and still have trusted God. Falling into temptation and trusting God simultaneously may seem strange to us. Nephi doesn't try to put himself into category A or B. He puts the sentences together deliberately, because trusting God as a human is a complex path. He is trying to eke out a life with God in which he knows he will fail even when he is trying to live into it fully.

In so much of Nephi's story he is battling the external elements of his family dynamics and the natural environment. These words give us a glimpse into the internal struggle he has also waged. Here we witness Nephi battling Nephi. He is maturing into a place of self-reflection.

2 Nephi 4:20

It is interesting to note that sometimes prophets will make reference to what God has done in the past in order to speak to God's actions in the future. It's like they keep a running resume of God's acts. We, too, should keep a record of how God has moved in our lives so that we can say, "This is how God has brought me through in the past. That is why I will trust God in the future." When things look incredibly hard in the moment, it might be good to hold our personal record of how God has carried us through our wilderness and preserved us through our own waters of the great deep.

2 Nephi 4:21

It's interesting to consider whether we have a record of this moment, when Nephi was so intensely filled with God's love, or whether Nephi is referencing something that was not recorded on the plates. We have discussed previously how Nephi's body is so reactive to spiritual experiences. He has written about his joints aching with grief for what his people left behind in Jerusalem.[2] Was this the same moment? The ability to feel grief for one's enemy is certainly an act of God's love. Or maybe it was another, unrecorded moment, like when he held his babies in his arms or when he helped his parents through death.[3]

2 Nephi 4:23-35

Watch for the exclamation marks in these series of verses. Don't miss the emotion in Nephi's words.

Nephi is incredibly hard on himself in this text. He berates himself, asking why he lets himself be tempted and why he feels grief and anger. He's not giving himself any space for normal human emotion and behavior. It's almost hard to read because he is pushing himself so hard to not feel all of the emotions that are okay to feel. Anger is more than a reasonable reaction toward men who have deliberately and repeatedly harmed him and his family. Grief is natural with the loss of a parent. Yet the manner in which Nephi writes it appears there is little time to grieve before he has to gather his family and leave under threat of violence. He does not have the luxury of attending to his grief and emotional health. So while we may want to give Nephi time to be still and have space for his emotions, his reality is that he has to return to refugee life. That is the story of any people who have to keep

---

2. 1 Nephi 19:20

3. While Nephi isn't specific about what moment he is describing, we should be specific in our own accounts and ask ourselves the question: When has God filled me with God's love?

moving to stay alive, including the story of the Mormon pioneers. People on the run will have to bury people along the way and get back on the road the next day. This is what Nephi is doing.

Nephi bears a strong resemblance to a Psalter in these verses. We should be reading this section in the voice of anyone who is fleeing danger, abuse, or violence. This is the prayer of those seeking safe passage. As you read these verses, imagine them in the voice of a Syrian father trying to get his children to a refugee camp. Imagine them in the voice of a woman leaving her domestic abuser in the middle of the night. Imagine them in the voice of a parent separated from her children after crossing an international border. This is a prayer of people seeking the safety of God in the low valley. Look for the number of phrases here that relate to leaving—path, deliver, walk, way, etc. This is about a dangerous journey and what it looks like to be forced to be on the move in search of physical safety. Putting these words into the mouths of the most vulnerable of our day underscores the fear and uncertainty that Nephi felt. It also reveals our responsibility toward those people today. May we be the hands that help God protect those searching for safety in the low valley.

2 Nephi 5:1–4

This is one last physical threat to Nephi's life before his final estrangement from his brothers. Nephi barely touches on this peril; he seems to be ready to conclude this much drawn-out abusive relationship.

It's interesting to note the anger that Laman and Lemuel have toward Nephi and the reasons they give behind that anger. There is a sense of entitlement to leadership that has created particular conflict for them. They say that they don't want Nephi to "be our ruler; for *it belongs unto us*, who are the elder brethren, to rule over this people," (emphasis added). Because their culture assigns them the privilege and the assumption of power, they are unsettled by Nephi taking leadership. They cannot understand how a younger brother could be called by God to lead them. There is a strong theme through scripture of a prophet called from an unexpected place and people being upset by how that goes against the established hierarchies of power. Frequently, the counter-cultural movement is through a younger brother being called—Cain and Abel, Jacob and Esau, Joseph and his brothers. In other cases, assumptions about socioeconomic or familial status are challenged. When Jesus announced himself at the temple, the men around him wondered how a carpenter's son could possibly claim to speak for God.[4] Christ's words made those men so angry that they, like Laman and Lemuel, tried to commit murder. So it's a critically important theme to understand what happens when people think they are entitled to certain positions of leadership and power. Notice how the belief of entitlement to power affects the different ways the brothers react to their conflict. All three brothers feel like they are burdened by this relationship. Nephi takes the path of walking away. Laman and Lemuel choose to attempt murder. Belief in our own privilege and entitlement can incite feelings of defensiveness when preconceived notions of power are challenged, as in the case with Laman and Lemuel.[5]

---

4. Luke 4:21–28

5. One of the most important lessons from scripture is that God calls unlikely people as prophets and leaders. We can depend on God to overturn the status quo or the social norm. Again and again, God upsets the hierarchies and structures that humans build to keep certain people in a place of privilege. The more calcified our beliefs of entitlement are, the more angry and violent the reaction is to that privilege collapsing.

If we are seeking to follow God, we must be open to challenging preconceptions about who ought to speak and lead. We need to be carefully questioning who our culture claims is faithful and who our culture directs to have a voice. If we are so stuck in our own narratives of power that we cannot hear a prophet called from the most marginalized groups in society, then we will miss God's word because we are too proud. Do not make Laman and Lemuel so distant from our own experience that we reject the authority of voices who have been traditionally silenced or passed by. When people from marginalized groups speak truth to power, we need to carefully examine our own reactions. Because if our first instinct is an urge to silence that person, that's dangerous. That will move you to kill the Messiah or murder your brother. Interrogating the sites where we are privileged with a voice is an uncom-

The final point to take away from these verses is the way that physical, emotional, and spiritual violence are wrapped up together. Laman and Lemuel have physically punished Nephi many times. They have also attempted something more subtle but just as destructive: they have been trying to crush him emotionally and spiritually for a long time. When they revel in his confusion about how to fulfill God's commandment to build a boat, they are happy that he is feeling distant from God. When they question his ability to lead and attack him for speaking God's words, they are hoping to harm his confidence in who he is and his relationship with God. These are yet further proof of the spiritual abuse they enact on Nephi. They take happiness in his struggles because they feel threatened by the choices he has made and the spiritual path he has taken. A failure to see that people can have widely diverse and meaningful spiritual journeys, replete with struggle and failure, can lead to unwarranted and harmful judgment.

2 Nephi 5:7

Nephi's story is one of escaping Jerusalem to find safety in the promised land, only to return to the wilderness because of once again being in danger. This is the story of a refugee, where a person returns to a transitional status again and again because of evolving and recurring threats. Nephi never seems to fully settle anywhere. His children seem to do better, which is the typical story of immigrants. But for Nephi, even the land of promise will be a land fraught with struggle and pain.

2 Nephi 5:9

The Nephites seem to have chosen their new name deliberately and it reflects their state of mind. The naming of themselves as "Nephites"

---

fortable process. What do we do with that? What violence rises up inside us? What does that anger do?

denotes their newfound separation. It's certainly possible to argue that the strong division of communities and the labels/names they employ will lead to further discord. Yet their choice is understandable. They have lived through years of trauma, they are seeking to establish a new identity and begin again. Claiming your own identity after great suffering is a powerful and liberative act. Throughout human history, the self-naming of a people is a vitally important part of a community's path to liberation. The Nephites are saying: We have taken on a new identity and we have fundamentally changed as a people. We cannot go back to who we were before the family schism, before crossing the ocean, before wandering in the wilderness. We have changed.

2 Nephi 5:14

Very understandably, Nephi fears for his life and the safety of his people. He has been given every reason to fear harm from his brothers. But his reaction is to increase the potential for violence by creating weapons. The symbolism of this set of swords being made in the model of Laban's sword—a weapon that already has a bloody and problematic history—is clear. While we cannot know the road not taken, this moment feels like a turning point in the history that will unfold between the Nephites and the Lamanites. In fact, before the end of the chapter, we learn that "wars and contentions" have already begun. If weapons are created, it becomes likely that weapons will be used. Again, this is not to say that mobilization was not necessary given the violent relationships of the brothers. Yet the preparation for war creates a certain kind of cultural climate among the people, and this should be noted.

2 Nephi 5:18–19

The language here is a little confusing, so it may be difficult to understand what's happening here. What is implied is that the Nephites ask Nephi to be their king and he refuses, saying he doesn't need to become their ruler because he already did that before the family schism. He seems almost afraid of becoming king, not because it may lead to an abuse of power, as other Book of Mormon prophets will state, but because the first time he tried it there was a threat to his life. Nephi is going into a place of deep pain here, remembering how he did what God asked of him in becoming the king and then had to flee from his brothers. Fulfilling divine revelation led to one of the most dangerous episodes of his tumultuous life. And these are the verses leading up to one of the most disturbing passages of the Book of Mormon.

2 Nephi 5:21–25

This section of the Book of Mormon is difficult. Nephi's anger and racism is laid bare and his words are distressing. Getting to a productive place with these words takes some time and a great deal of effort. In further examination there are some factual errors to Nephi's claims, based on what Nephi has already written. In verse 24, Nephi writes, "And *because of* their cursing which was upon them they did become an idle people, full of mischief and subtlety."(emphasis added) And yet we know that Laman and Lemuel were idle and mischievous *before* their skin supposedly darkened, when they were in white skin. From Nephi's account, we have observed Laman and Lemuel engage in extreme violence, attempted murder, laziness, disobedience, and cruelty all while inhabiting white skin. Nephi's claim that one followed the other simply doesn't follow what we already know about this family. It's not coherent. Nephi is not seeing clearly; he doesn't recognize that Laman and Lemuel did so much of their unrighteous activity in what he saw as light skin.

The second claim that doesn't ring true is that the Lamanites were idle. Nephi contrasts the Lamanites with his own people, who were "industrious."[6] This appears to be true, as the Nephites built

---

6. 2 Nephi 5:17

a complex society with government, cities, a military, and long-distance communication. Yet we will read in the following pages of the Book of Mormon that the Lamanites build a society that rivals that of the Nephites. Out of the wilderness, the Lamanites also manage to construct a government, cities, a military, and a flourishing community.[7] Nephi's proof of his own people's industry also seems to apply to the Lamanites. As the text provides evidence that contradicts Nephi's assertions, there is room to doubt his objectivity, and to consider that the text records the diatribe of a man who is deeply traumatized and speaking from his hurt and rage.

The final claim here that is strange, given Nephi's own account, is his condemnation of the Lamanites for hunting in the wilderness for food. We know that Nephi used his bow to hunt for food and that God guided him in those efforts. Why is hunting for food suddenly a sign of immorality?

Carefully examining these claims together leaves the reader wondering what is lying beneath the surface of Nephi's angry accusations and socially constructed racism. It appears that post-schism, Nephi continues to resent and fear his brothers and their families. This is understandable, as Nephi endured so much trauma at their hands and his people begin to battle with the Lamanites almost immediately after the separation. Nephi seems to be taking that lingering resentment and building a case against the Lamanites. He is reframing the narrative, attributing their behavior to skin color when his account states otherwise and pointing out every possible trait he can criticize. It's such a universal human reaction that we can understand Nephi's hurt. Nephi's vitriol reveals the grief he has never finished processing.

Readers can reasonably give Nephi space for his feelings. Unfortunately, Nephi makes the mistake of attempting to enlist God by pronouncing the Lamanites people cursed by God. Nephi's feelings

---

7. See a few of the many references to the Lamanites' cities, communication, military, and culture in Alma 23:4, Alma 52:2, Alma 58:2, and Mormon 2:4.

of anger and resentment are real and warranted. Even expressing that through constructing a narrative of how the Lamanites are less desirable and lazy is still somewhat understandable considering Nephi's state. But Nephi does something more destructive: he couches his anger in theology and claims that God has cursed the Lamanites. Seeing God's punishments in other people's lives is a very dicey thing to do and humans are not particularly good at getting it right. It would, after all, be easy for an observer of Lehi's family to see years wandering in the wilderness, living in tents, eating raw meat as evidence of God's displeasure toward Lehi.[8]

Nephi's effort to have God's approval on the lingering effects of his own trauma is deeply destructive. Nephi chooses not to limit his pain to his personal journey. The moment he takes his disgust and deep hurt and decides to stamp God's name on them, he enters into theologically dangerous territory. It is not okay to weaponize a prophetic call. Serious harm can come from not being able to separate personal bias and feelings from the Divine. Those who follow God need to be to recognize and separate their own prejudices, their own racism, their own sexism, their own homophobia from the Divine. As humans, we share these tendencies, and must continue to resist the urge to throw God's name around in an effort to endorse prejudice and discrimination.

Nephi's words present readers with two simultaneous challenges: offer empathy for his humanness and refuse to elevate his words to the divine status. Nephi made a mistake. We should not compound the problem by turning it into a foundation for our own theology.

2 Nephi 5:26

There is a subtle but important message in the sequence of this verse following directly after the previous section. In verses 21–25, Nephi is

---

8. We know from the New Testament that lepers were considered cursed and that Jesus Christ upended that claim. The same thing is true for the woman with the issue of blood and the man who was blind and deaf. Humans are simply not good at correctly identifying the objects of God's wrath, so we probably shouldn't try it.

in a place of emotional devastation. And in that moment, he is organizing the structure of the church. At the beginning of this church, three of its leaders—Nephi, Jacob, and Joseph—are still processing their own trauma. In the previous verses, Nephi isn't maligning just his own brothers. He is cursing their children and all their descendants. The church is established in the middle of some deeply problematic theology about how God views Laman, Lamuel and their progeny. It follows on the heels of this language of hatred, and we know from the pages to follow that it plants a seed that will have ripple effects of harm down the generations. Founders do not always know how they are bringing their own burdens and biases when they lay the foundations for a work. No church can be established outside of our own human experience. But we have to at least be cognizant of the narrative by which we started a church and address how that ripples down. Because we have the ability to look backwards and forwards through the records of the Nephites and the Lamanites, we have a responsibility to recognize how Nephi's hurt causes further harm.[9] The deep harm takes shape in maligning and degrading an aesthetic and/or phenotype. Nephi does not just talk about his brothers' character flaws, the real issues, but dangerously links them to their skin color, hereby planting the seeds of discrimination within this community both socially and theologically.

---

9. The Nephites never seem to truly and openly address the theology that Nephi introduces in this chapter. Yet it is hard to believe that these words of hate and anger do not play a role in the war and hatred that follows this people. A church that has never addressed these words that were spoken at its founding will see the consequences bubble up again and again. Just because a wound goes untended does not mean it goes away. This is the lesson we can take from the Nephites: the Church of Jesus Christ of Latter-day Saints also had Nephi's words at the time of its organizing. Unless we are willing to sit with these words, allowing ourselves to feel the discomfort, and wrestling with what these words mean, Nephi's broken theology will continue to cause harm.

2 Nephi 5:27

It sometimes feels like scripture doesn't give us enough about the manner of happiness. Nephi's story is one of years of deep trauma and grief. It would be nice to give us some time to sit in the happy years a little longer. Our longing for narratives of joy is a good reminder that we need to tell our own stories of peace and laughter along with the stories of struggle. There is great meaning in a life lived in the manner of happiness.

2 Nephi 5:34

Underlying this rapid overview of forty years is the fact that Nephi, Jacob, Joseph, and their families never truly get rest from Laman and Lemuel. Even separating the families does not mean that they can set down the relationship. The conflict escalates into outright war between the people. For Nephi, that means that his entire life is circumscribed by his brothers. That's a fact that we should take into consideration when we examine his feelings toward them.

2 Nephi 6:1

Nephi is still alive as he hands off the record to Jacob for a time. We often think that there's one single prophet during a given era in the world, but scripturally that isn't the case. Many times in the Book of Mormon there are multiple prophets living at once.

Unlike Laman and Lemuel, Nephi does not see his younger brother as a threat. Laman and Lemuel took offense at their younger brother being called as a leader and a prophet, adhering to the sibling age hierarchy of their time. Nephi is able to have a very different relationship with his younger brother. Jacob speaks as a prophet to the people and his record is included as authority in the plates. The fact that Nephi was able to not only turn away from the social power structure of his time but also refrain from recreating the abuse that was heaped on him is indicative of his strong character and connection to God. While at certain times things come out of Nephi's mouth to show how hurt and angry he continues to be because of the trauma he experienced, he is at least able to heal enough to willingly share power with his younger brothers.

2 Nephi 6:3

Jacob writes that he has great anxiety for the Nephites. This tells us that Jacob is walking into the uncomfortable role of a prophet. Prophets always seem to have great worry for their people. It seems that they cannot love a people so deeply and have divine call and not have a great amount of concern and lament—this is why so many prophets through scripture seem to be in sorrow. Jacob worries for the souls of the Nephites.

2 Nephi 6:9

This is a beautiful description of how scriptures work. Jacob is reading the record of the Israelites and through that study, God is moving him toward inspiration and revelation for the Nephites. And because Jacob makes a record of that, readers of the Book of Mormon can both understand Jacob's journey with God and receive personal revelation for themselves. In this way, scripture is a communal experience, as we read others' narratives and use those stories to have direction in our own lives. Yet Jacob also emphasizes the intensely individual aspect of scripture and revelation here. He explains that study and exegesis of scripture is a personal effort, repeatedly writing the word "me," as in "God has shown me," to emphasize the individual journey with God. With the communal and the individual aspects taken together, a divine force connects us to the ancestors of our faith. Our relationship with scripture is multilateral, not bilateral. As they both journey with God, readers and writers of scripture connect to one another, separated only by time and geography. Jacob is showing us how to use scripture. "God has shown unto me" empowers readers to know that God is still moving through text with God's people.

2 Nephi 9:2

Any time someone invokes the phrase "lands of our inheritance," readers ought to be somewhat skeptical. An endless promise of ownership of land that is steeped in theology often does not turn out well. The three Abrahamic religions are very tied up in divine rights to land and historically an enormous amount of violence has followed. We need to be very careful about what we have decided God wants us to possess. We need to be even more careful about how we are taking action on what we deem is a divine promise. There is a big difference between believing that God has promised a people land and employing violence to enforce that promise. Whenever a reference to divine inheritance is used, it's useful to ask the text, "Is this claim to land/power/position being used to justify violence?"

2 Nephi 9:5

Readers should always note when they are introduced to another name for God. "The Creator" is yet another wonderous name for God. God as Creator.

2 Nephi 9:6–8

It's unusual in scripture, including in the Book of Mormon, to name the devil as an embodied being rather than a generalized evil threat. However, invocations of the Fall are an exception to that. When discussing the Fall, the devil is a corporal being who has direct effect on the actions of humans. Yet authors of scripture reference evil in their own times as something vague and distant, even when describing truly evil acts such as war and genocide. It's a bifurcation, where we take the devil out of evil because that evil sometimes shows up in ourselves. We can name the devil very clearly in a narrative as distant as Adam and Eve, but we don't want to name contemporary evil as being rooted in the devil. Those who wish to follow God will have to sit with the discomfort of the human propensity for evil.

2 Nephi 9:17–20

Along with giving God praise for being just, merciful, and holy, Jacob shares his definitions of justice, mercy, and holiness. He calls God great because God "executeth all his words" and God's laws are fulfilled. God is great in mercy because God delivers the righteous from Hell. God is holy because the Lord "knoweth all things, and there is not anything save he knows it."

Two points emerge from these descriptions. The first deals with the invocation of justice and mercy. To acknowledge that God is great in both of these things is to embrace paradox and contradiction. It is in the push and pull of the seemingly irreconcilable differences between justice and mercy that the true greatness of God reveals itself.

Secondly, Jacob's description of God as holy because of omniscience is puzzling. He is equating holiness with infinite knowledge, which is not how prophets usually describe holiness. Jacob's definition of holiness here is more revealing of Jacob's values than anything else. We can tell through his recitation of text and his way of speaking that he is academically inclined. He seems to revel in the words of scripture and has spent time and effort in the study of it. So for an intellectual prophet, God is holy because God knows all things.

2 Nephi 9:23–24

What does perfect faith look like? Faith is imperfect in its nature. It is holding onto things that we have not seen and believing in things that we do not know. Why would God require a perfect faith? No part of our salvation has ever been dependent on us being perfect. While in Bible study we can dig into potential multiple meanings of words or possible mistranslations, in the Book of Mormon we can't follow linguistic traces. For a biblical reference to the word "perfection" we can look at the word in Hebrew and understand that one meaning is "mature in thought and action," which would be a fitting interpretation for this text. But we don't have scholars of the reformed Egyptian text used on Nephi's plates, which leaves us with a phrase—

"perfect faith"—which does not seem to make sense or fit with other scriptural definitions of faith.

At first glance, verse 24 seems to simply be the inverse of verse 23. Verse 23 states what people ought to do to be saved; verse 24 states that if they don't do those things, they will be damned. However, Jacob runs a risk in his writing, because these two things are not the same. Cursings and damnings are not the good news. Employing language of confidence about who will find grace requires caution. Anything that divides the beloved community or disconnects us one from another deserves strict scrutiny. Jacob may not be wrong here, but, as readers, we can insert a mental note about human fallibility whenever the author is cursing or damning in the name of God. It is easy to extrapolate God's words to more than what was intended. If God says, "Here is what a person should do," it is easy for the listener to flip that and say, "If you don't do these things, you're damned," but this is a logical fallacy. Confounding these two ideas can lead us down dangerous paths of being confident that we know another person's eternal future.

Humans have a tendency to try to tame God, to attempt to bind God to a certain checklist, ignoring the scriptures that show us that God breaches laws and spills over expectations in a million different and unexpected ways. Jacob has already glorified God for being simultaneously just, merciful, and all-knowing. We cannot expect, in our human capacity, to narrow the scope of God to something that we can understand. We ought not to believe that we can know who will receive God's grace. Trying to predict God is like trying to predict the weather. We may get some things right, but something will always surprise us.[10]

---

10. It's worth noting that in verse 35, Jacob unintentionally highlights the way God makes exceptions to seemingly unbreakable laws. The edict to not kill another human is constant throughout scripture. Yet Jacob's own brother, Nephi, deliberately killed Laban. That story is complex and difficult for many readers to understand and accept, but it shows how God upends expectations again and again.

2 Nephi 9:30-37

Jacob returns again and again in this section to the dangers of two of the great indicators of social status: wealth and education. He takes pains to make clear that education is good, as long as it does not become idolatrous. As stated before, Jacob is clearly educated himself—he can quote long passages of scripture and take listeners through a complex exegesis. He is also brother to the king and presumably one of the elites of the Nephite society. So this focus on wealth and education is not an exhaustive list of things that may stand between us and God, but rather topics that seem particularly relevant to him. It is fair to presume from his history and his words that wealth and knowledge are things that he has struggled with in his efforts to remain humble before God. Jacob approaches his record so cerebrally that it can be difficult to get a sense of his personal and spiritual life. But we never want to separate the prophet's words from the prophet's own struggles. Prophets will always have the lens through which they are journeying with God. The things that are in their hearts will reflect that journey.

2 Nephi 9:42

At the end of the Book of John, Peter sees the resurrected Christ on the shore while Peter is fishing from his boat. He jumps into the water, apparently out of joy in seeing Jesus and an eagerness to be with Him as soon as possible. Anyone who has watched someone try to hurry through water knows how ridiculous it looks—the person attempts to move rapidly and yet is slow and off-balance and the result can be funny to watch. But this is what Jacob is asking us to do when he calls us to be "fools before God." We should be so excited to be with God that we drop any pretense of dignity and rush to be with God. Any social conventions or ambitions that constrain our yearning for the Divine need to be left behind. This is the crux of all of Jacob's warnings about wealth and knowledge—that we need to be careful of anything that lends us the consequence in our own eyes that hinders a wild and unruly chase after God.

2 Nephi 9:44

At the end of chapter 9, Jacob makes a sudden pivot. While he has heretofore been academic and deliberate, he now becomes passionate and personal. He repeatedly calls the people "beloved," emphasizing his emotional connection to them. He moves from being just the authority or the teacher to being a part of the beloved community. Divine call must be rooted in love for our people and a sense of being inextricably tied to them. Jacob also makes himself vulnerable here, using imagery of being naked before the people. Taken with verse 14 about the righteous standing confidently in robes of righteousness, Jacob seems to be voluntarily placing himself, unprotected, in the midst of the people.

Jacob is also explaining his own accountability before God. Prophets have a responsibility for their people. Even when they are reluctant to speak, they are often called to do so. Nephi wrote that he was "constrained" to speak to his brethren. Jeremiah said it was like a fire shut up in his bones.[11] Prophets may feel so connected to their people that they feel like if they do not speak, then they are guilty. Their people's sins will collect on their clothing unless they "shake them" through giving the people warning and guidance. In our own lives, God may prompt us to tell our families, churches, and communities that something is not right. That is deeply uncomfortable at times because it makes us vulnerable. But we are tied to one another, so there are times that we cannot be silent because God will hold us accountable.

2 Nephi 9:45–54

At the end of this day's sermon, Jacob moves away from his logical explanations of theology and into an emotional, personal space.

---

11. Jeremiah 20:9

First and foremost, his people are beloved. But they must shake off the chains that bind them because sin has consequences. And then comes the magnificent invitation to feast on God's word. He reminds them that to partake of the richness of the gospel, the only requirement is desire. This section is so full of energy and excitement about the word of God. Jacob closes the day with an incredibly hopeful, joyful voice.

2 Nephi 10:2

Once again, the Nephites have a prophet who appears to have foreseen the demise of their people. The connection Jacob draws here between the physical and spiritual is an intensely strong one. Jacob is claiming that unbelief can have physical ramifications. His "nevertheless" statement—that God will be merciful and many will be restored, speaks to the power of perspective in narrative. Where a narrator chooses to end a story decides whether a story has a happy conclusion. If the Book of Mormon ended the story of the Nephites during the time of Samuel the Lamanite, the narrative would be one of sin and death. If it ended at the time of Jesus' visit and the period of peace, readers might see a story of redemption. Ending with the collapse of the Nephite civilization and Moroni's wandering gives a sense of grief. Then again, if we take an eternal perspective, we might see a story that is ultimately one of restoration with the Divine. Readers don't know exactly which slice of history Jacob is speaking to here, but the important point is that perspective affects how the story is told.

2 Nephi 10:3–4

Readers need to be wary any time there is a maligning of an entire people. The statement that only the Jewish people would reject and crucify the Messiah deserves strict scrutiny. Does this seem like a reasonable claim? Even a cursory review of evil in the world makes it seem unreasonable. If we take seriously Matthew 25:40, in which Jesus says that any harm we do to the most marginalized of society is the same as harming him, then in a very real way any society that has turned its back on the vulnerable has harmed Christ. If we take this view, then there are few societies in the history of the world who would not fall into the category of those who would hurt or even kill their Messiah. A society like that would appropriately be called Zion. So we need to walk away from this idea that Jews were particularly more evil than any other group of humans.

Why does Jacob make this claim? While we cannot know his thoughts, putting his words in the context of his life is revelatory. Jacob was born in the wilderness to parents who had been forced into refugee life because of the violence of the people in Jerusalem. His early life was full of suffering and he witnessed his family's years of hardship. Unlike Lehi or Nephi, Jacob has no personal connection to Jerusalem—he never lived there and doesn't have any people he loves there. His entire narrative is that it was a place so evil that it completely disrupted his life because the people tried to kill his father. Just the fact that Jacob uses the term "the Jews"—as a people separate and apart from himself, is revealing. Jacob does not associate himself with his parents' people. They are not a part of him. His refugee status and the suffering that came from it has ceased any connection that he might mentally make with the Jewish people. With that context, it's no surprise that Jacob's vision of the crucifixion of Christ seems, to him, to be the result of the most wicked civilization in human history. Given the history of his life, it seems like a response that readers can understand and forgive.

2 Nephi 10:9

There is beautiful parallelism in this verse, as kings become nursing fathers and queens become nursing mothers. Men and women together are nurturers. Jacob makes it clear that there is no degradation in kings and queens becoming nurses; it is part of being royal. In fact, it happens because "the promises of the Lord are great." Succoring, nurturing, and tending are the greatest work that women and men do.

2 Nephi 10:10–13

The way land is discussed here is problematic in a couple different ways. The issues involved with the idea of land as divine inheritance were discussed in the section about 2 Nephi 9:2 and will be further discussed in this chapter.

The Americas are also described as "a land of liberty." This is generally interpreted as a promise kept, that the United States has divine claim to being a land of liberty. Reading the text this way is deeply harmful to people who historically and currently have not experienced America as a land of liberty. The United States has been a land of liberty for some, not for all. Perhaps Jacob's prophecy does not reference the United States at all; there is nothing in these words to say that Jacob is speaking about any particular country. Or maybe it's a promise unfulfilled, dependent on certain conditions that have never yet been met. There's a great deal that's unclear here, but readers cannot pretend that all people have found the United States to be a land of liberty.

Interestingly, in the midst of all this language of inheritance and power, there's a cross current of dominance and breaking down borders in verse 13. Verses 12 and 13 seem to directly contradict each other, with verse 12 claiming that God will take sides in national conflict and verse 13 stating that God stands only against anyone who fights against Zion. Verse 12 tries to place God on one side of national boundaries; verse 13 places him entirely outside of human borders. Verse 13 tells us that anyone who does evil will perish, without regard to nationality or any other socially-constructed category.

2 Nephi 10:18

This verse sounds similar to what Nephi told Laman and Lemuel in 1 Nephi 22. The essence, in both cases, is that there is this intensely complicated relationship between the Nephites and the Gentiles. In one verse, Jacob says that the Gentiles will afflict the Nephites and "be like a father unto them." It's easy to imagine a listener to

Jacob's talk being confused. As we wrote with Nephi's words, communities are complicated. They may simultaneously offer blessings and scourges.

2 Nephi 10:19

"It is a choice land . . . above all other lands." Why does Jacob insert the land being better than all others? Wouldn't it be enough to simply state that it's a choice land? This may seem like a small, insignificant insert, but it is dangerous theology. It puts the speaker into an adversarial relationship with his fellow humans, creating a competition for God's love. Words that prompt ideas of hierarchy or divine preference lead us to ideas of scarcity rather than abundance. We know that "all are alike unto God"[12] and "the earth is full and there is enough and to spare."[13] There is no reason to try to claim a place as the most blessed or the most loved. It's an unnecessary phrase that moves us into a place that is not conducive to an all-loving Divine.

There is an additional danger with this language, and that is revealed in the syllogism of the verse. Jacob writes that "it is a choice land . . . above all lands, wherefore I will have all men that dwell theron that they shall worship [God]." If the land had been inferior, would the inhabitants have a lesser invitation to come to God? If the land decays—perhaps because of a natural disaster—does God love the people less? This is a precarious place to set down one's faith. Tying one's faith to "God has given me the best land of all" is dangerous because it's too easily undone.

2 Nephi 10:20

There is an interesting shift in inheritance here that points to "inheritance" being more dynamic and less rigid than is usually understood. Jacob writes that they "have been driven out of the land of our inher-

---

12. 2 Nephi 26:33
13. Doctrine and Covenants 104:17

itance; but we have been led to a better land." Although people in scriptures repeatedly insist on their claim to a specific inheritance, their stories repeatedly indicate that no one should become dependent on the idea of receiving their inheritance. Repeatedly throughout the Old Testament, the older son ends up ceding the birthright to the younger son. Lehi's family loses their inheritance when they follow God. The message is clear: do not expect to receive an estate simply because of when and where you were born. It does not belong to you. God may replace it with a different inheritance, but that new inheritance may be hard-earned and painful. God's idea of inheritance pushes back against our social system of power and rights.[14]

2 Nephi 10:21-23

The phrase "broken off" appears seven times in the Book of Mormon and all of them come from Nephi or Jacob. This is unsurprising, given how the family's exile plays such an important role in their spiritual narrative. These verses are beautiful and can give comfort to the many people in the world who have been broken off from their people, church, community, or family. God remembers all who have been broken off. God remembers all who have been disconnected, who have had to leave out of fear for their safety. Jacob places himself in community with all the other broken-offs. They are

---

14. In scripture, inheritance is dynamic and meant to be uprooted. People in scripture, just like people today, are so wedded to the idea of what they're destined to have that they struggle to accept their new inheritance. There is a certain amount of grief work that has to be done as people let go of what they believed to be theirs and accept their new situation. It sounds almost like a miscarriage, where the expectant parent has to give up on their expectations for what they thought was theirs. In some ways, it seems that is what is happening when Jacob repeatedly writes, "This is the best land. This is better." It sounds like a personal reassurance that they can accept the loss of their inheritance. He is working toward convincing himself and his people that the shift in their inheritance is for the best. While this is human and understandable, the healthiest path would be acknowledge the loss while simultaneously being grateful for the new land. One land doesn't have to be better than the other. We can simply appreciate what we have and what was lost.

his people.[15] Jacob reminds those who are broken off, cast off, hanging their heads, and driven out of their inheritance to cheer up their hearts, because God remembers them. It is comforting to recognize that God remembers these people as they are in a place of vulnerability and grief.

2 Nephi 10:24–25

Who knew that praise for God and grace are partners? The phrasing here is stunning—grace divine instead of divine grace, as if grace is modifying the word divine. Jacob seems to be saying that it is only through grace that we even see God's miracles, that we are capable of giving praise. Grace is not only the final gift we need in order to be restored to God's presence. It is foundational to having a relationship with the Divine at all.

2 Nephi 11:3–6

Nephi is using the words of Isaiah and Jacob to "prove" that his own words are true. The word prove is interesting. Modern-day usage typically associates it with evidence or facts that could be admitted in a court of law; "prove" can also be used to mean test or try, as it is used in the Old Testament.[16] "Proving the dough," when making bread, refers to the time when the bread is left alone to rise, proving whether the yeast is alive and working. With this definition, Nephi

---

15. Mormons recognize and celebrate their own period of being broken off through Pioneer Day and pioneer treks. That tradition of respect for a time of exile is admirable. But remembering our own history of being broken off can also prompt us to consider who is struggling with being broken off today. Once a group has shifted from being pioneers to being accepted in the mainstream culture and having social power, memory work should not just be a time of memorial. It should call us into a state of community with those who are in social exile now and prompt us to help them know that God remembers them. While retelling stories is good, Pioneer Day ought to be more than just a celebration.
16. For example, Exodus 16:4 or Deuteronomy 8:2

may be inviting readers to test or try the words[17], not claim that they are incontrovertible. Rather than thinking of "proving" as the end of the discussion, we can use it as an invitation to "experiment upon [the] word."[18]

2 Nephi 11:4-6

Nephi has had a hard life. We have just a few more chapters of Nephi's own words before the record is handed over to Jacob for good.[19] What does Nephi find delight in at this time in his life? His soul delights in speaking to people of Christ, keeping covenants with God, and wondering at the grace, justice, mercy, and power of the Divine. He finds joy in sharing the good news. That's a beautiful example for all of us.

2 Nephi 25:1-2

Nephi is one of the oldest people in his community, and one of the few with any memory of Jerusalem (the only exceptions would be any unnamed and unheard women about whose existence the record is silent). He has a choice about how much of his culture to pass on to his people. He writes here that he has made a very intentional choice to not pass on much of anything, even the good things, including how to interpret and understand Jewish scripture. Nephi is so traumatized, so hurt from the violence of his youth, that he completely rejects the people of his childhood community. He doesn't just filter out what he saw as dangerous or unhealthy, he walks away from all of it. Here he explains the loss this choice creates for his community: because understanding Isaiah requires cultural and historical knowledge, his people cannot understand their holy books. Their spiritual lives are less rich because of his lingering pain.

---

17. Paul echoes this idea in 1 Thessalonians 5:21.
18. Alma 32:27
19. The first handoff happened in 2 Nephi 6.

There are two interesting points here, one particularly about Nephi and one about understanding scripture. The first is that the way Nephi remembers and writes about the Jews sounds a lot like the way he writes about the Lamanites. He doesn't see nuance in the people who have hurt him and his family. He pushes away from them so hard that in his mind, they are representatives of all the evil in the world. Seeing complexity in people who have committed deep acts of violence is a privilege of having time and resources to heal. Nephi never had that. He is a deeply traumatized person and so he is willing to reject an entire people, even at the cost of missing things that would have benefited his descendants.

The second is that despite Nephi insisting that the words of Isaiah are plain, he reveals how difficult it is to explicate scripture without knowledge of history, language, and culture. He refers to "the manner of prophesying," indicating that not all prophesying is going to look the same. There is a context to prophesying that helps make the words more accessible to readers. The further removed readers are from the original author, the harder it is to make the meaning and intention clear. Nephi had the benefit of growing up in Jerusalem and receiving an education in Jewish scripture, so Isaiah is clear to him. Without those benefits, the same words are unclear to his people. It is understandable that people today, being removed even farther from Isaiah's time and place, struggle even more.

2 Nephi 25:4

Choosing to not pass along a limited knowledge of Jewish methods of interpreting scripture puts Nephi in a difficult place, because he wants his people to understand Isaiah but he doesn't want to pass along the cultural tools for understanding Isaiah. His way of getting around it seems to be to insist that knowledge is unnecessary because all they need is the Spirit. This is a little unfair. While spiritual inspiration is, of course, critical to learning from the scriptures, Nephi moves into a place of blaming his people for not understanding something that they are unprepared to understand. It's harmful language and Nephi is blinding himself to his own privilege of education. The very first sentence of the first verse he writes in the Book of Mormon tells readers, "I was taught somewhat in all the learning of my father." He received a religious education from his father. Now he emphasizes that understanding comes through spiritual enlightenment, as if his education were irrelevant. He doesn't see that Isaiah is plain to him because of the groundwork that was done for him. Calculus may be plain to those who have majored in math, but that doesn't mean that calculus is easy for everyone. Anyone who has had the benefit of education and then turns around to those who haven't had that benefit and says, "Why is this hard for you—it should be obvious," is actually harming those they wish to teach. It leads to people giving up because they believe that they, instead of the system around them, are failures.

2 Nephi 25:13-15

Nephi jumps directly from the violence that Lehi experienced in Jerusalem (v. 10) to the crucifixion of Christ in these verses, underlining how he links the two in his head, despite those events being more than 500 years apart. He's using what he knows about the life of Christ to further convict the Jews, who he already sees as evil because of his own experiences. Interestingly, Nephi skips any reference to the birth or life of Christ. We have a record of the vision Nephi saw of Mary and that the angel described her in the most flattering language. In Nephi's rush to condemn the Jews, he skips over the fact that the Messiah was born to and found family and community with the Jews. Mary was a Jew. Joseph was a Jew. Elizabeth, Zachariah, John the Baptist, and all the disciples were Jews. We don't want to miss all the good people who are part of this society simply because Nephi harbors lasting scars from his past.

All this language about destruction, gathering, and scattering does not sound particular to the Jews, although Nephi seems to see it that way. It is the human condition for individuals and communities to wander and return to God. Nephi's own descendants will do it again and again in the coming years, but Nephi does not make that connection between his people and the Jews. Although he knows what the future holds, he does not seem to see that the Nephites are just like the Israelites in the way that they experience periods of righteousness and immorality. This is an opportunity to make a human connection between two groups of people; instead, Nephi uses it as additional evidence to push farther away from his heritage.

2 Nephi 25:23–30

Nephi seems to be explaining to people why they following a law that will be replaced. Nephi is uniquely situated as an Old Testament prophet who knows about the higher law that Christ will bring. He seems to have some discomfort with the law even while knowing that the Nephites need to continue to follow it, so he tells them to be obedient even while hinting that the law will become irrelevant. Given Nephi's efforts to separate his people from the Jews, even going as far as not teaching them the Jewish methods of interpreting scripture, it's fair to infer that he fears that his people will follow the same path as the Jews. This section reads like Nephi is afraid that his descendants might react to Christ in the same way as the Sadducees and Pharisees, so locked into the law that they miss the Messiah in their presence. Nephi seems to be trying to warn the Nephites that the law is a means, not an end. It exists to bring people to God, not to become an idol in itself. For readers today, Nephi's warning is still relevant: don't let your focus on the law prevent you from living the gospel.

2 Nephi 26:3–6

Not for the first time, the land acts as an additional character in the Book of Mormon. Here, the ground seems to carry a witness of the violence acted out upon it and helps to carry out the punishment as well.

2 Nephi 26:7

Again and again, Nephi returns to the anguish he feels about the future destruction of the Nephites. He invokes it even more often that he references the violence that he personally endured. It is the great grief that hangs over the rest of his life. And yet he still feels compelled to admit to God "Thy ways are just." Nephi is an extraordinary example of faith in the face of a life of terror, suffering, and sadness.

2 Nephi 26:9-10

The writers of the Book of Mormon have a tendency to speed through periods of righteousness at lightspeed. Periods of peace are not a focal point of the text. Nephi refers to three generations of a Zion society in one sentence. Fourth Nephi is only one chapter long. For whatever reason, Nephi and Mormon agreed that this time did not need further documentation or exploration. There is a loss there. While modern day readers know what a violent and sinful society looks like, it's hard to imagine one in which an entire civilization walks in cooperation and faith. In times of desperate sadness, it is moments of human connection and kindness that give us the hope to press on. The construction of the Book of Mormon sometimes doesn't lend itself to offering the hopefulness that people need in living out the gospel.

2 Nephi 26:15-21

The profound message of the gospel is that every individual voice matters. Ultimately, no one is silenced by death. The very earth will give power to the voices of those who have been ground into the dust. In a way, the description here of voices rising from the ground is terrifying. These voices will be familiar to us. Those who have pushed others into dust will have to listen to their voices convicting them. Any question of whose voices will rise from the dust is made clear in the end of verse 20: the poor, whose faces have been ground into the earth.

Verses 20–21 are a warning to anyone who believes themselves to be safe with God because of their participation in a church. The great stumbling block of the Gentiles is their pride from having "built up many churches," while they "preach up into themselves their own wisdom" even as they do nothing for the poor. If a church focuses on size and power instead of on helping marginalized people, then it will face God's wrath. These verses are an indictment against any church that professes to have a God but that has not taken care of "the least of these." If a religion has many churches, it ought to be vigilant in making sure that it has done enough for the poor. Verse 21 goes even further: many churches actually cause envyings, strife, and malice. This is a wakeup call for church goers. Churches will have to accept a lot of accountability for their teachings. If they have not done enough for the poor in their communities, they will have to listen to voices rising from the dust, convicting them for their failure to truly live the gospel. All of us who profess faith need to read these verses seriously.

2 Nephi 26:25–28

Having already invoked churches, Nephi now expands his language to include synagogues and any "houses of worship." Not only is his invitation to the gospel universal, his vocabulary emphasizes true inclusivity. By using such broad phrasing, Nephi signals that this message is truly for everyone: those who attend churches, synagogues, mosques, or any other house of worship. None are forbidden.

This invitation is vital and the way it is given is so important. Nephi writes that the sweetness of God is available *without price*. There is nothing that needs to be done to receive it except to show up at the table. Religions sometimes act as if the grace of God is transactional and that it can only come to those who have been baptized or pay tithing or show their commitment in some other way. There are no barriers to God. The invitation is without limit.

2 Nephi 26:29

Jesus Christ taught that his followers should be "the light of the world."[20] The exact same phrasing here, 500 years before Christ lived, seems purposeful. Nephi's words add clarification to Jesus' exhortation to be a light: those who set themselves up as a light for the purpose of getting gain and praise but do not seek the welfare of Zion are practicing priestcraft. This underlines the earlier point in verse 20: anyone who builds churches or spreads the message of the gospel but does so for their own interests is internally rotten. Any church that does not do everything it can to alleviate the suffering of the poor is hypocritical. In other words, it is not enough to be in the business of growth. When a church focuses on merely expanding membership while not lifting up the oppressed and proclaiming the gifts that God offers without price, it walks in perilous territory.

2 Nephi 26:33

The entire second half of this chapter is a warning directed specifically at churches. Churches are warned to not turn anyone away because the gifts of God are free and open to all. Churches are told that priestcraft is when someone teaches the message of the gospel for the purpose of their own gain. The overarching message is clear: churches must beware of actions or words that place a barrier between a person and God. There is no social category or life circumstance that prevents a person from being worthy to sit down at God's table. Churches risk God's condemnation if they prioritize their own growth and power over inclusivity and charity.

Read in this context, verse 33 takes on additional meaning. While we can take from it counsel that individuals should avoid sexism, racism, classism, and any other social hierarchies, it is primarily a reminder to churches that they do not have a monopoly on grace. God invites all. There is no price. No one is excluded. Even those who do

---

20. Matthew 5:14–16

not recognize Elohim or who have no faith are remembered by God. This universal invitation to partake of the goodness of God comes with no strings attached. All are welcome is a powerful invitation.

One final note about verse 33: Biblical scholars point to the use of merism in the story of the creation.[21] Merism is a rhetorical device in which two ends of the spectrum are named as a way to encompass the entire spectrum in between. In Genesis, this means that God created the light and the dark, but also every point of dawn and dusk in between. God created the earth and the firmament, but also every place between the seas and the stars. God created males and females, but also every person who identifies as bi, trans, non-binary, or queer. The two points encompass the spectrum, they don't exclude it.

Merism also seems to be employed here. God welcomes not just black and white people, but also every shade of pink and brown skin in between. God welcomes slaves and those who are free, but also every person who lives in conditions like poverty or debt that make them only partially free. For Nephi, Jew and Gentile are the two ends of the religious spectrum. But just to be clear that even that spectrum includes everyone, God adds that non-monotheists are also welcome. Every social division of Jacob's society is disrupted by God embracing the spectrum of human life.[22]

2 Nephi 28:1

The following chapters are the last prophecies we will receive from Nephi after we've followed decades of his life. He's grown from an

---

21. Adele Berlin, Marc Zvi Brettler, and Michael A. Fishbane. *The Jewish Study Bible*. (Oxford University Press, 2004).
22. If modern-day readers were to create their own list of categories used to divide people into disparate camps, what would it look like? We would probably add heterosexual/homosexual, transgender/cis-gender, and immigrant/citizen, among others. Regardless of which groups are named, the message is the same: All are alike unto God. As taught by Dr. Anathea Portier-Young at Duke Divinity School in Fall 2013 Old Testament course.

unsure young man to a visionary who built communities and leads his people. This last section of his prophetic witness deserves careful reading.

This isn't the first time that Nephi has written about the Spirit constraining him. In 2 Nephi 4:14, Nephi was constrained to speak to his brothers. These two incidents of the word constraint, as well as the fact that Nephi strongly argued against becoming king, hint at Nephi's reluctance to lead.

2 Nephi 28:3-4

These verses include one of the many warnings to churches contained in the last few chapters of 2 Nephi. Claiming exclusive rights to God and then using that to contend against other churches is not acceptable. This is a crucial message for any religious body. Do not treat God like a scarce resource to which only you can lay claim.

2 Nephi 28:5-13

The first step of corruption is for churches to argue with one another. The following verses give two additional possible steps down the path away from God. First, churches may teach that God's work is done and God has given all power to humans. Anyone who claims that God's miracles are done is teaching false doctrine. Secondly, churches may teach that there won't be any serious consequences to sin, that grace and forgiveness come easily: "Following the commandments is a waste of time because God will forgive everything." Both of these paths are ways in which people may claim they have no need of God.

Why did the theology become corrupted? Verse 12 tells us that the first step down these other paths is pride. Pride leads to false teachers and false doctrine. Reference back to verse 3—the first step of this path of corruption is saying "I am the Lord's." The problem is not in claiming to have truth or to have a relationship with God. The problem is when pride prompts us to claim a totality of truth or to battle against other churches.

2 Nephi 28:13–15

Many people read scriptures with a lens of seeing themselves as part of the few, as the ones who are "the humble followers of Christ." Instead, we can strive to read scripture in ways that allow the text to convict and inspire us to bravely name our brokenness and identify how we have fallen short in our relationship with God and neighbor. By allowing the scriptures to move us to repentance, we let the text live in ways that call us to a deeper and more profound discipleship.

2 Nephi 28:18–24

There is an interesting parallelism in the language of verse 19. Those who belong to the kingdom of the devil[23] will be stirred up. They will either be stirred up to repentance or they will be stirred up to anger. Many will react to the collapse of their wealth and privilege with anger. That is the fruit of entitlement and pride. Throughout scripture, prophets (including Nephi's father) barely escape with their lives because their words stir up anger and violence. People who have internalized their own goodness—"I am the Lord's church"—resent having their religiosity challenged.[24]

---

23. i.e. the great and abominable church. In this book we've defined that church as any people or organization that prioritizes amassing wealth over lifting up the poor; see this book's section on 1 Nephi 13.

24. What would it look like if the Savior came into every church today and said, "You got things wrong. You're not as faithful or as good as you think"? Our response indicates where our commitment is truly rooted. Is our faith in God or in our church? Could we handle God telling us that our religion has not been Christlike? Verse 24 ought to make all of us worried. Are we at ease in Zion? Do we believe that we are the few who never take part in the great and abominable church? These verses say that Zion is not well. God is holding up a mirror to the body of Christ and asking us to honestly see where we are sick and afflicted.

2 Nephi 28:30-32

The repetition here that God gives us knowledge gradually is important. God, at times, bestows knowledge in increments. For all of our studying, searching, and pondering, we know just a small amount of God's truth. We're just getting very small pieces here and there. The phrasing indicates that God gives all people small amounts of knowledge. It may look different with different people because teaching with God is not limited. The method that we've used in our own learning does not exclude the many other ways that other people may learn truth. We are better off acknowledging that God has an expansive array of pedagogies.

Following prophets and clergy does not mean unquestioning obedience. Use caution when trusting a human who speaks for God. If you feel that they are moving with God, then you can trust them in this capacity at this moment. Just because someone has been moved by the Holy Spirit in the past doesn't mean that they will always speak and do what is right. If we know anything about the prophets in scripture, it's that they have moments of glory as well as moments of terrible mistakes. They are broken humans, operating in the human experience. The only being who should have our unwavering faith is God. That puts more responsibility on each individual to be continually asking for guidance. But expecting or believing that any person will not move in and out of the Spirit is very dangerous and hard on one's faith.

After all these warnings, there is a final concession to the inevitability of failure and the offer of God's grace. The Gentiles will ultimately fail. Yet God's arm is wide enough and long enough to catch the whole world. The overarching message of this chapter is that while humans are smaller, weaker, and less knowledgeable than we think, God is a lot bigger, more merciful, and gentler than we think, so it will be okay. There will be many times that we will get our theology wrong. Knowledge will come slowly. But put your trust in God because God will sustain you.

2 Nephi 29:4-5

This is a lovely calling to remembrance of those who have sacrificed in the past to preserve the records and testimonies of God. It's also an interesting juxtaposition to Nephi's previous language about the Jewish people, such as in 2 Nephi 10:3-6. Understanding the gap between these two sections of scripture may rest on the fact that 2 Nephi 10 is Nephi writing his own interpretation, while 2 Nephi 29 appears to be words directly from the Lord. It's a useful example of how prophets sometimes let their own biases influence their theology.

2 Nephi 29:7-14

"Know ye not that there are more nations than one?" could be written on all holy texts. This is the radical idea that the Book of Mormon witnesses of: there are more nations than one. The Israelites were not the only people who received God's word. It's easy to read this chapter as being about Christians who, satisfied with the Bible, reject the Book of Mormon, and stop there. But it has the potential to be so much more revolutionary in its theology. What if, instead of seeing these verses as a condemnation of Christians for limiting their scripture, readers took these words as a directive to not limit our own minds to the ways that God has spoken and will speak to people all over the world? Today, we can transpose Nephi's question and move it forward: "Know ye not that there are more nations than two?" Why should our holy texts be limited to the Bible and the Book of Mormon?

This chapter has the potential to emphasize that message and to motivate its readers to see more clearly that God does not belong to one people or one book. Believers in the Book of Mormon know what it's like to have other people dismiss their sacred text. Too often, we turn around and do the same to others, insisting that with the Bible and the Book of Mormon we now have all the scripture we need. The Book of Mormon is not a one-off, an outlier of Christ's work in the world. God moves throughout the world. Christ has sat with and taught and blessed and performed miracles with people in the places we least expect. We can seek out these times and places and eagerly adopt their stories as part of our own canon. What would it look like for us to take seriously Joseph Smith's repeated injunctions to embrace truth wherever we may find it?[25]

The very existence of the Book of Mormon is radical in its testimony that Christ visited with and spoke to people outside of the Middle East. One of the main purposes of the book is to stand as a witness of the expansiveness of God: that God speaks in unexpected places, to people that are unknown to the rest of the world. The Book of Mormon stands as a lighthouse of how God's work can move within and throughout the great diversity of the human experience. Verse 8 speaks to this as being one of the purposes of the book: "Know ye not that the testimony of two nations is a witness unto you that I am God, that I remember one nation like unto another?"

Verses 9–10 contains God's response to anyone who tries to regulate who has God's word or dictate when or how God speaks. God's work is not yet finished. Everyone has more to hear. We can substitute any holy book for "Bible" here—God is not finite. No book contains all of God's words.

Verse 11 is an important verse in the Book of Mormon because it frees us up from thinking that we have a monopoly on truth. It liberates Christians from believing that they are the only ones holding knowledge and replaces it with a web of God's truth that spans the globe. Every follower of God is part of a huge beloved community, one that holds truths and powers that we may not yet be able to imagine. This is an opportunity for an incredible connection to all of

---

25. For example, Joseph Smith's letter to Isaac Galland, Mar. 22, 1839, Liberty Jail. Published in *Times and Seasons,* Feb. 1840, pg. 53–54: "The first and fundamental principle of our holy religion is that we believe that we have a right to embrace all, and every item of truth, without limitation or without being circumscribed or prohibited by the creeds or superstitious notions of men, or by the denominations of one another, when that truth is clearly demonstrated to our minds, and we have the highest degree of evidence of the same."

God's children. But when you decide that your truth is limited to you and your canon, then you have decided to disconnect yourself from the other words that God has spoken to other peoples. God is saying here that we should know that we are not as isolated as we think.

Just in case readers of the Book of Mormon are inclined to think that these words are only for those who are limiting themselves to the Bible, verse 12 makes explicit the message that there are many books of scripture. The Jews will write their account. The Nephites will write their account. The other tribes of Israel will write their account, "and [God] shall speak unto *all* nations of the earth and they shall write it." (emphasis mine) All. God speaks to every nation, meaning that innumerable documents about how God has walked with humans exist. Every one of them has yet another line, another precept, another little bit of truth that we can embrace.

Eventually, everyone will have all the holy words. It's thrilling to think of the day when all of God's children will sit down together and say, "Tell me about how God has been moving among you. Tell me your sacred stories. What has God been doing with your people? What miracles have you seen?" To know that all of that truth and wisdom will be brought together into one unabridged volume is awe inspiring.

2 Nephi 30:1–2

Nephi helpfully indicates here that the account is switching out of God's word and back into Nephi's voice. These verses tell us that there's one deciding factor about whether we're in good standing with God, and that's whether we have repented. Anything about chosenness or covenants matters less than whether we are striving to live righteously.

2 Nephi 30:6–7

How does Nephi reconcile the way he writes about the Jews with the words of God in the previous chapter? This language about "scales of darkness" and becoming "a pure and delightsome people" is disturbing. Once again, the only way to understand it is to understand Nephi's history of trauma that may account for his prejudices.

2 Nephi 30:12-18

Just as how the language a person uses to describe God often says more about the person speaking, so the way a person describes Heaven or Christ's second coming can also reveal their deepest desires. As someone who has too often been a victim of violence, a person who has had to flee for his life, a boy who lived in fear of his brothers, Nephi envisions global harmony as his ideal world. The predators and the prey set down their roles and live peacefully together. The most vulnerable people in society—children—are repeatedly assured of their safety. No one is trying to hurt anyone else. As we come to the end of Nephi's life, we see a man who seems worn out with the struggles of his life. What he yearns for is rest and peace.

2 Nephi 31:2-3

Once again, Nephi uses the word "plain" to describe his written prophecies. Yet his description of "plain" in verse 3 doesn't quite match how we would typically define the word. Nephi writes that his words are plain because God adapts God's words and teachings to the language and understanding of people. In other words, God meets us where we are, according to our culture, education, and experiences. That doesn't mean that doctrines are simple or easy to understand, as we might guess from the word plain. It means that they are accessible. Nephi's words are simple for him because God spoke to him in Nephi's language, culture, and education. That doesn't mean that Nephi's words will be easy for readers to understand today. But it is important to know that God speaks your language, too.

2 Nephi 31:13

The ability to speak with the tongue of angels is invoked repeatedly in this chapter and the next. What precisely it means is unclear at first, although we can appreciate the poetry of the phrase. In scripture, angels come shouting praises, sharing joyous news, explaining something critically important, bearing truths, and sometimes giving warning. But in 32:3 Nephi makes the phrase clear: "Angels speak by the power of the Holy Ghost; wherefore, they speak the words of Christ." So the promise given here is that those who are baptized and receive the Holy Ghost will have the ability to speak the words of Christ. That's a powerful promise when we consider the roles that angels play in scripture.

2 Nephi 31:16–21

The idea of enduring to the end is very particular to the Book of Mormon. Nephi gives a long list in this chapter of boxes that must be checked in order to attain salvation. Taken together, it's a steep set of requirements and Nephi seems to be confident in the inflexibility of the list. This is black and white understanding of a God who, throughout scripture, tends to break a lot of rules. God has been known to contradict laws, customs, and edicts. The way Nephi writes about things that *must* be done or a person *cannot* be saved is perhaps too limiting for a God who upends our expectations and mandates. We have to be careful with phrases that bind God too tightly. It may be distressing to us if things don't happen in that certain, precise way. Words or doctrines that are too rigid bind us to the concept of an inflexible God, when God is often far more surprising and unruly than our own narration. Interpreting scripture in a way that describes a rigid God gives us a theology that doesn't allow for the way God upends our ideas of what "should" happen.

Nephi writes repeatedly of a strait and narrow path that leads back to God. Of course, the word strait means narrow, providing additional emphasis on how narrow the path is. Fiona Givens has argued that the path is so narrow because it is limited to one person: the person walking that path. Each person walks their own individual path back to God and no one can share the path of someone else.[26] Nephi has walked his own circuitous, convoluted path toward the Divine and many times he has felt deeply alone on that journey. He knows very well how narrow the path sometimes feels. When we use this interpretation, Nephi's words in verse 21 sound full of compassion rather than judgment: "And now behold, my beloved brethren, this is the way; and there is none other way nor name given under heaven whereby [humans] can be saved in the kingdom of God." Nephi is telling them, "Your way may feel very narrow at times. It will be hard. Your faith journey may feel lonely and exhausting. Just press forward with faith."

"Feasting upon the word of Christ" uses an interesting verb, one that Nephi and Jacob have employed multiple times in their narratives. A person sitting down at a feast is not capable of eating all of every single dish. It would not be possible or good for the body. To feast requires action in the form of ingestion. It also requires agency as we choose which dishes to eat and how much to take. It's not an intravenous drip, a passive experience that comes upon us with no effort or awareness. Feasting upon the words of Christ requires us to be a part of the process.

2 Nephi 32:4–5

The scriptures are full of invitations, even injunctions, to ask questions of God. Joseph Smith was unafraid to ask big, hard, seemingly unanswerable questions. This ought to embolden us to ask if we don't understand, because God wants us to understand. Revelation does not happen in a vacuum—it consistently happens because people ask questions. We may not always like the answers and we may have to wait for a response. But we are encouraged to ask.

---

26. Public statement at the Miller-Eccles Study Group on April 13, 2013.

Saying that the Holy Ghost will "show unto you *all* things what ye should do" is a big promise, seemingly an unattainable one. But we also believe in a big God, with whom all things are possible. So this text may be true, and yet we need to be careful with it. We don't want to attempt to apply this promise to our own lives, which are complicated and unclear, and begin to wonder and have doubts about our own standing with God. This scripture isn't intended to shame people about whether their faith matches up to the promise. Sometimes we have to wait for an answer. Sometimes we pray and get silence. It's okay to name that tension. Nephi makes big promises about communication from God, but we also know that his pain and questioning was sometimes unalleviated. At times he had to act in faith. There are plenty of times that we will get an answer that is a non-answer. That's part of a journey with God.

2 Nephi 33:1

At the very end of his narrative, Nephi admits that he is uncomfortable with writing. He prefers speaking to his people and writes that when he speaks, he feels the Holy Ghost accompanying his words in the moment. This may seem surprising to the reader—Nephi has never acknowledged this discomfort before. But Nephi seems to have enjoyed the experience of the personal connection, being able to watch the Holy Ghost move in the moment. While readers may feel the power of the Holy Ghost as they study Nephi's words, Nephi isn't able to be present for that moment, so the experience feels inadequate to him.[27]

---

27. This small moment gives us a little unintended insight into Nephi's prophetic experience: writing this account was a struggle for him. He felt like he wasn't very good at it and he didn't enjoy it as much as preaching to his people. He was obedient to the commandment to make this record, even though he didn't know its purpose and therefore didn't know if it would make a difference to anyone. This pushes up a little bit on his earlier words about how understanding and following God is simple, because he is essentially admitting that one of the great works of his life—this record—was done on faith. This written record was not the optimal way that Nephi

2 Nephi 33:4-15

Our final words from Nephi speak to the weight of his role as a prophet and his love for his people. They encapsulate the paradox of the strength of his testimony of Christ with his personal shortcomings. In verse 4, he admits to his own weakness, yet continues to hope that his words will persuade the reader to do good.[28]

Nephi's love for his people has been one of the defining characteristics of his life. He has served them, worked to protect them, and preached to them. He has, at times, seen anyone who may threaten them as almost sub-human. There is a ferocity to Nephi's love for his people. In these last verses, he invokes that love multiple times. He speaks in concentric circles about his love: his people come first, then the Jews (because of his ancestry), then everyone else. This is an honest, vulnerable, frank testimony. His love isn't perfect and unbiased, but it is strong.

The very last phrase: "for thus hath the Lord commanded me, and I must obey" is an interesting comparison to 1 Nephi 3:7, where Nephi states that he will go and do the Lord's commandments. We can take together the words of the young man, which are full of zeal, and those of the old man, which sound more quiet and resigned. So much has happened between these two statements: a lifetime of pain and struggle. But what links the two is a commitment to obey the word of God. One of the most important lessons of Nephi's record is that he consistently tried to follow God's commandments. That is an incredible legacy.

---

would have wanted us to hear his story. Maybe if we had been able to sit down with him in person and hear his words, ask him questions, and dialogue together, the points of discomfort in his narrative (i.e. 2 Nephi 5) would have disappeared. Even Nephi feels that this is an imperfect way to share his journey with God. That makes it easier to offer him some grace for its flaws.

28. Once again, he is asking the reader to extend grace, because he has done his best within the limits of his knowledge and circumstances. No one should ask for perfection in the prophetic. It's unrealistic and inhumane. Nephi is admitting to his imperfection, just as many other prophets in the Book of Mormon will do.

JACOB

Jacob 1:2–4

With Nephi's death, the record enters a new period of time, one in which the people who lived in Jerusalem are dead or perhaps close to death.[1] The spiritual leaders of the Nephites are now Jacob and Joseph, who were born in the wilderness.

Jacob states at the very beginning that Nephi instructed him to "write upon these plates a few of the things which *I considered* to be most precious," (emphasis added). Just as other prophets will admit to the human filter of the Book of Mormon, Jacob states that he has to use his own judgment to decide what ought to be included in the record. That means that what we're getting in his narrative is one person's view of what is most precious. This is not necessarily the record that Nephi's wife or Jacob's daughter would have produced. There is subjectivity here. We are reading about what one man believes is most important. That doesn't make it any less valuable, it's just important to note that there is editorial work happening in this scripture.

---

1. We don't know Nephi's wife or any other women in the group, so it's impossible to know whether any other people in the society have a memory of Jerusalem.

Jacob 1:5–6

Although we often think of faith as antithetical to anxiety, here the two not only coexist, but actually work together. It was because of faith *and* great anxiety that the revelations are brought to pass. Faith working together with anxiety can be productive, spurring a person to ask questions but be patient and meek with the answers that come. Faith does not mean that we need to be absent of worry. Healthy anxiety—the kind that pushes us to take action—wielded with faith can be powerful.

Jacob 1:7

What does it mean to labor diligently among one's own people? This is still a small community—Lehi left Jerusalem just 55 years earlier—and they have likely heard the message of the gospel. But Jacob and Nephi want to make sure that the people not only hear the words, but actually "partake of the goodness of God." Partaking of that goodness means being able to enter into God's rest. So the goal of all of this diligent labor among their own people is that they follow God to a place of rest.[2]

Jacob 1:13–14

Here we get a glimpse into how these families splintered into different groups and how the narrative is going to mostly ignore that diversity. Each of these different -ites have separate origin stories of how they got there and those stories will affect their theologies. The Zoramites, for example, will come back into the narrative in Alma

---

2. Latter-day Saints are an exuberant people who have a strong work ethic. Our belief in eternal progression means that we sometimes overlook the need for rest. For those who have been oppressed in this life, eternal labor in the life to come may not seem like partaking of the goodness of God. Jacob is saying here that we will all have a period of rest. From a prophet born in the wilderness, during the darkest times of his father's life, we know that this life is hard enough that it warrants a divine rest at the end.

with the Rameumptom and a very different culture and faith than that of the Nephites.³ Yet Jacob frankly states that he's simplifying the narrative into two separate groups—just the Nephites and Lamanites. That makes the story easier to understand, but it comes at a cost. Whenever we make something that is complex into something that is simple and binary, we lose the capacity to see nuance. There will be a difference, in the coming narrative, between the people who are descended from Jacob and those coming from Zoram and those coming from Lemuel and those coming from Ishmael. Yet because Jacob lumps them all together, the reader is forced to refer to "the Lamanites" without always knowing exactly who is being referenced and what their history is. It negates the reality and complexity of the origins of the people. Also, taking away someone else's name is always risky. Jacob is writing a record about another people, without their input, and giving them a different name from what they call themselves. That's not good policy. All people have the right to name themselves. Jacob's oversimplification makes it easier for the writer and reader, but there's a loss in the process that we need to acknowledge.

Jacob 1:15–16

The following chapter will go into greater detail about the sins of the Nephite men. It's important to note here how the treatment of women and the desire for wealth are interconnected. The common thread is accumulation: the men want wives like they want gold, as commodities that reflect their self-importance. Once again, we see how those who thirst after wealth trample vulnerable populations under their feet in an effort to get what they want. Jacob's speech at the temple will underscore that point further.

---

3. Alma 31

Jacob 2:3

It's not unusual for Book of Mormon prophets to start out a rebuke with some form of the statement, "You know that I am doing the best that I can." They are effectively inviting the people to call them out if they're acting in hypocrisy. These prophets can use tough language in calling people to repentance because their people know that they have labored diligently in their callings. For Jacob, that motivation to work hard stems, at least in part, from anxiety.[4]

Jacob 2:4-6

By Jacob's account, the Nephite men have been strictly obedient to the law (verse 4) but are not following God in their hearts (verse 6). This should tells us that obedience can be a performance. Checking off a list of commandments alone does not make us right with God. We are accountable for our innermost thoughts as well, which are more difficult to discern than our outward deeds.[5]

Jacob 2:7-9

The people are gathered at the temple and Jacob feels inspired to rebuke the men for their actions. The women and children are also present. At first glance, it may seem strange that the women have

---

4. It may not be possible to truly labor in one's community without feeling anxious. If you have the call to bring goodness and God into your community, it comes with worry and frustration, because you will see how you and your people are failing. Perhaps that's why Moses struck the rock—not that he worried about God, but that we worried about how his people were working with God.

5. The role of prophet is an office with a great deal of power that could be easily abused. Jacob says he knows what is in these men's hearts, even though their actions are in line with the commandments. A prophet needs to be able to say, "This may look right, but it isn't right," because of the fact that outward obedience is not the totality of our spiritual lives. But being able to claim a knowledge of someone's interior life is a serious responsibility. Those who are in the role of the prophetic need to use a heavy amount of discernment and caution when they walk that road. And we all need to have a healthy skepticism of anyone who claims to tout that power.

to sit through this meeting. After all, Jacob states at the beginning that this sermon is not for them and that hearing the words will cause them additional pain. As Jacob acknowledges, these women are in a vulnerable place and they came to hear healing words for their wounded souls, not to be confronted by the failings of their husbands, sons, and fathers. So why doesn't Jacob confront the men in private? The answer, it seems, is accountability. By stating these words in front of the women, Jacob is making the men accountable to their wives. The women have to sit through painful words, but Jacob is wielding his power to bring them some authority and justice. That is a radical action, given that the Nephite culture seems, like other ancient cultures, hierarchical and patriarchal. Jacob is willing to shame the men in front of the women and children, an action that levels the power structure. There is a subtext to his call for repentance, one in which people with more social power are being held accountable to those with less.[6]

In contradiction to those who say that words are harmless, Jacob finds nothing wrong with being able to be wounded by words. In fact, he praises the women for being tender and delicate. While being strong and slow to take offense is good, we also need to remember that there is merit in someone who can be wounded simply by words. Jacob knows that words can be daggers, especially to someone who is already hurting and vulnerable.

---

6. Women being further harmed in situations that are necessary for men to be held accountable ought to sound familiar to modern readers. Victims of sexual assault who are able to get law enforcement to prosecute often have to live through the additional trauma of a courtroom just to bring justice to their abuser. There is the initial wounding and then the further harm that happens just to make things right. In these cases, the wounded may appreciate the words of accountability even as it carries additional hurt. The women in this chapter may have needed the prophet to call their men to repentance and name them as accountable to the women and children, but that doesn't mean that it's a joyful experience. How to avoid additional harm while providing justice to the wounded is something we still have not figured out how to do.

Jacob 2:12–13

At certain times in the scriptures, we take "brethren" to mean everyone, including women. In other cases, such as in this verse, "brethren" appears to refer literally to just the men. This is the problem with using male-gendered pronouns to refer to everyone: it burdens women with the work of sorting through when they are included and when they are not. Men are able to see themselves everywhere. Women have to read with the additional work of interpreting whether the message is intended for them. This is why gendered language matters.

The land of promise is described here as a blessing from God, something intended to continue to provide for the people for generations. And yet the people have exploited the land by using its abundance to achieve great wealth and then persecute the poor. How we react and what we do with blessings that God has promised us matters. Just because something has been given to us doesn't mean that we can do whatever we want with it. It's possible to exploit the blessings of God. When we take the blessings God has given us and become greedy and prideful, we are turning the "hand of providence" against other people. There is a delicate line to walk between being grateful to God for what you have and claiming that God gave you those things because you are special. It is the deadly element of pride that creates the caustic belief of entitlement to blessings. It is pride's ability to turn the most beautiful things—"the hand of providence [that] hath smiled upon you most pleasingly"—into toxic things. Pride allows us to weaponize the providence of God.

Jacob 2:16–20

Pride metaphorically resides in our hearts because we think of hearts as being the place of intentions, the feelings and emotions behind what we do. With pride, we need to ask ourselves hard questions about the motives behind our actions. Pride can affect our internal lives without changing our outward behaviors. This leads to hypocrisy, where a person may look righteous but have an ailing soul. On the other hand, pride can also corrupt behavior that is otherwise not bad. The problem for the Nephites is not necessarily that they sought after wealth, but that they did so with the intention of lifting themselves up over their brethren. Verse 19 indicates that seeking after wealth in itself is not wrong. The problem is when our hearts are wrong—when the motivations behind the action meant to elevate ourselves over another.

Verse 17 gives us the answer to the pride of our hearts: "be familiar with all and free with your substance." This is gorgeous. First, be familiar with all. Look around you and see what folks need. Be familiar with the need. This is not a blind giving; a person needs to be in community to know what the needs are around them. This is a call to relationship with those around us in order to know how to give of our substance. Be familiar with all, without discrimination or limits. Secondly, we are called to take the thing that we seek and bestow it on others. The gospel is not natural—it asks us to do things that are counter to what we think or expect. We find God by taking all the things that we want, that we're striving for, and giving them up. Our own freedom comes when others are rich like ourselves. This is part and parcel of liberation theology: we are not truly free, we cannot find salvation, while others are oppressed.

Our first priority must be to "obtain a hope in Christ." Then we can seek for riches, but it must be with the intent to do good, and that good looks like giving it away. "Clothe the naked, . . . feed the hungry, . . . liberate the captive, and administer relief to the sick and the afflicted." Whatever blessings come to us in the form of wealth or privilege must be given up to the least of these. Seeking after riches must be done with the goal of alleviating suffering and canceling burdens through moving people back into the community by being open and generous.

Verse 20 gives us a final note on pride. Pride drives us to injure one another. It is not a victimless sin. It will always move to injure others around us. Pride destroys community. So while pride can come between us and God, it also affects our ability to love our neighbors. In this way, pride threatens our ability to follow both of the first two great commandments.

Jacob 2:22-23

In verse 22, Jacob concludes the first half of his sermon by telling them that he wishes that the pride that is corrupting their souls was the worst of their sins. In verse 23, he begins to explain what is even worse than what went before: the Nephites are manipulating scripture to excuse their own sinful behavior. They are weaponizing holy text in order to justify committing evil. The gravity of misusing scripture for our own selfish purposes is perhaps underrated. It's also likely more common that we realize. The common theme throughout this chapter is how people take God's blessings (in these verses, a land of promise and scripture; we can expand that to any of God's great gifts) and turn them against others. Jacob is condemning the people for asking God to back their evil as they use scripture to justify themselves. His role as the prophet is to correct the mishandling of text, to tell the people how it has been abused.

Jacob 2:28-29

Given the rest of this text, it's fair to assume that the Lord delights in the chastity of men as much as the chastity of women. We don't need to make this all about women's virtue because God clearly cares about the unchaste nature of the men's behavior.

Verse 29 is interesting as a comparison to verse 12. In verse 12, the land was full of promise. Just 17 verses later, the land may be cursed. This is how blessings can be corrupted, according to the way we move in them. The same things that bless us have the ability to indict us. When the Nephite are prideful and try to justify our bad behavior with the backing of scripture, their blessings may turn on their heads and instead become a source of misery.

Jacob 2:31-35

These verses are some of the most overtly feminist messages of the Book of Mormon. Jacob is saying that what is worse than the corrupting influence of pride is the way the men are treating God's daughters. There is a kind of claiming in the repetition of the word daughters—these women are not just people, they are God's daughters. God hears the sorrow of the women and it stands as a witness against the wickedness of the men. God led God's daughters out of Jerusalem. Jacob does not write that God led Nephi and Lehi out of Jerusalem and the women followed. This is a direct relationship between God and the women of this community. This further interrupts the narrative we've been given, in which women play an essentially silent and passive role. God led the daughters out. Women are directly in two-way communication with God, as God hears their cries and leads them with revelation.

There is also a repudiation of men weaponizing intimacy here. Jacob gives a sense of the responsibility men have in these sexual relationships. Throughout history, women have borne the blame for both consensual and non-consensual sexual encounters. We blame women for what they wore, where they were, and what they said that somehow compromised them or invited men to take advantage of them. Jacob's indictment of the men pushes up against the sexist narrative that women are inherently responsible for sexual relationships. Jacob is clear: Nephite men are responsible for their own behavior, and the way they have treated women is unacceptable.

Finally, we cannot miss verse 35, in which Jacob runs counter to all of Nephi's talk of how sinful the Lamanites were. The Nephites may believe that they are superior to the Lamanites, but Jacob is telling them they are actually in worse standing with God for how they treat the women of their community. For all of the faults of the Lamanites, at least the Lamanite men treat their women with dignity. This message will be further expanded upon in chapter 3.

Jacob 3:1-2

Jacob takes a brief break in his chastisement to offer words of consolation to the Nephite women. While he was previously speaking specifically to the men, it is fair to assume that the complete shift of audience here means that Jacob is now addressing the women and children. Just as it was important that Jacob rebukes the men in front of their mothers, wives and children, it is equally important to note the specific language Jacob uses to console the women in front of their husbands.

He references the need for "firmness of mind" twice in these two verses, alluding to the fact that there's something about being in the midst of injustice that warrants the blessing or prayer of a firm mind. This is the only place in the Bible or Book of Mormon where this phrase appears. The phrase seems particularly important when readers consider the challenge of being firm of mind in the face of husbands who are trying to use scripture to justify abuse. Jacob is encouraging the women and children to stay firm in the face of deep harm caused by the Nephite men.

Jacob also promises the victims that they will be consoled in their afflictions. God comes to us in the midst of our troubles. If we are suffering from the wrongdoing of others, we can go to God and say, "This is not our fault, this is not our doing, we live in an unjust world. Console us." If we pray with faith, we can receive that consolation and God will plead our cause. God takes over and becomes our advocate, sending down justice where it is needed.

Besides praying for firmness of mind and receiving consolation, those who are pure in heart but suffer from injustice can feast on the word of God. We don't reflect enough on how God's word can be pleasing to the soul. A feast is diverse abundance, with a multiplicity of options for how and what to eat. So God's love has an abundance that supplies all variations of need.

The briefness of these words of consolation may seem as if Jacob doesn't care about those who are suffering. Readers may sometimes wish that scripture spent more time on comfort and less on condemnation, but it's important that these short couple of verses simply direct people back to God. Jacob is essentially implying that the pure in heart don't need him, they only need God. At this moment, the prophetic word is needed in denouncing evil in society, but Jacob reminds them that God sees them and will give them all the comfort and consolation they need, and they can bask in the love of their God.

Jacob 3:5-7

These verses are a critically important addendum to Nephi's words about skin color and sin.[7] Here Jacob makes two fascinating statements: 1) he indirectly separates skin color from righteousness by telling the Nephites they have offended God more than the Lamanites and 2) he states that the Nephites hate the Lamanites because of the color of the skin, effectively identifying the Nephites' prejudice and racism.

At the beginning of verse 5, Jacob writes that the Nephites hate the Lamanites. That in itself is startling—the almost casual way he mentions that they have broken the commandment to "love thy neighbor as thyself" points to how violent and cruel this society has become. Not only do the Nephites hate the Lamanites: they hate them because of "the cursing which hath come upon their skins." And yet the Lamanites are more righteous than the Nephites. Jacob's reproach addresses the Nephites, or those who are said to be "fair and delightsome," and their belief that they are superior to the Lamanites. This verse is deeply entrenched in social justice work and seeing the Book of Mormon as a place to delve into how racism, classism, sexism, and other forms of prejudice have been with us for a very long time.[8]

---

7. For example, 2 Nephi 5
8. Remarkably, the language that Jacob uses here is almost identical to the language that white supremacy uses today: claims of "filthiness" should sound familiar to

Interestingly, even Jacob doesn't seem entirely ready to engage in the deeper conversation addressing the Nephites' hatred. He condemns them for their whoredoms and he undercuts their belief in their own superiority, but he doesn't delve into the racism and hatred that is prevalent in the community. We can't know the reasons for this, but it likely stems from Jacob's place in an ancient culture that is tribal and insular as well as his personal history of suffering abuse from his brothers and being a student of Nephi. He has a lot personally wrapped up in the antagonism of the two peoples and it's very difficult to call out what you are experiencing yourself. His human experience seems to somewhat limit his view of how this community is offending the Divine.

Jacob acknowledges that the Lamanites are not a righteous people—he writes that the Lamanites have observed "*this* commandment" (note the singularity). The Lamanites have their own problems and failures. And yet they are in better standing than the Nephites *because of how they treat the women of their society*. Verse 7 lays this out even more clearly: the men treat the women with dignity because their relationships are rooted in love. This one piece of their culture has ripple effects in their society strong enough that Jacob writes that the Lord "will be merciful unto them; and one day they shall become a blessed people."[9]

Several things happen in verse 7. Jacob compares the hatred of the Lamanites for the Nephites with that of the Nephites for the Lamanites. He has stated earlier that the Nephites hate the Lama-

---

modern ears. The modalities by which we carry out oppression may have changed but the ideas that lie beneath them don't change very much. Hate speech looks the same over long stretches of human history. For further scholarly work as a reference, please read Ibram Kendi *Stamped From the Beginning: The Definitive History of Racist Ideas in America* (Lebanon, IN: Bold Type Books, 2017).

9. We know today that societies in which women have protected rights and an equal standing are more stable, less violent, and more prosperous. Jacob's words indicate that was just as true in ancient times. An entire community is elevated by women being treated with dignity.

nites for the color of their skin. Here, he writes that the Lamanites hate the Nephites "because of the iniquity of their fathers." Hatred is inheritable! The Lamanites were taught to hate; it was woven into the daily lives of their children. And Jacob's words give us a small hint of where the blame lies when that happens: at the feet of those who taught the hate. He offers the Lamanites just a little bit of grace because of what they inherited from their parents.

Jacob spends a significant amount of time in this chapter comparing the Nephites and the Lamanites. In important ways, this is incredibly unhealthy and ultimately damaging. It is not an effort to create beloved community. A parent who says to a child, "If you aren't obedient your sibling is going to get all of your toys" will not foster a healthy relationship between the children. It models a worldview of scarcity, in which there is a limit to God's blessings and cursings and people are in competition to receive or avoid them. And yet we see this kind of mentality throughout the Book of Mormon and the Bible. If we are wondering why nations continue to pit themselves against others today, we should look at how our sacred texts repeatedly name one against the other. God is bigger than that. We need to step outside the idea of who is up and who is down, who is more righteous and who is less, and instead approach God with the question: "How can I and my people do better?" The Nephites will have to answer for what they have done with what they've been given. The Lamanites will have to answer for what they have done with what they've been given. The kingdom of God is built on our own community's relationship with God, not so much where we stand in comparison to others.

Jacob ultimately reaches that place with his final question in verse 7: "[W]herefore, how much better are you than they, in the sight of your great Creator?" That's probably the humbling question that we each need to ask ourselves when we are trying to create hierarchies before God: "Are you better than them in the sight of God?" The answer is no, because all of us approach God as sinners in need of grace.

Jacob 3:8-10

There are deeply harmful things said in these verses, mixed with some lovely things. Don't be afraid to separate them out. We can hold prophets accountable and recognize the bad that sometimes comes with the good. Sometimes our holy texts can do toxic work even in their goodness.

The way Jacob repeatedly associates filthiness with dark skin and whiteness with righteousness is not okay. We need to recognize the damage that this pairing does—it feeds unrighteous thoughts and ideas about skin color and human worth. This language hurts people. Jacob is unaware of how his own prejudice is seeping into his theology. And yet, he's attempting to offer grace. He tells the Nephites to remember their own filthiness rather than revile the Lamanites. He is creating a grace that is marred with discrimination and shadowed with contingencies. Even as he strives toward the Divine, he carries with him his own human frailty.

Verses 9 and 10 remind the Nephites to remember their own filthiness. Jacob is willing to point out the filthiness of the Nephites, but notice that the phrase doesn't come in conjunction with the color of their skin. Only the Lamanites have their skin color associated with their negative behavior. This is subtle but critically important. We can infer that the Nephites are filthy in their whiteness but in their case, their behavior is treated as separate from their skin color.

They are not convicted for the color of their skin in the way the Lamanites are, yet their behavior is, Jacob says, worse than that of the Nephites. So you can be as white as you can be, and yet still be worse than the supposedly filthy dark-skinned people. Jacob doesn't quite reach this understanding—his language indicates that he still mentally associates filthiness with dark skin—but we need to understand this. We need to see how this pattern is replicated in our own society, where brown and black bodies are punished disproportionately because they are associated with criminal behavior.

As verse 10 indicates, generations are entangled in their racist ideas. The examples of parents may grieve their children. There's a big emphasis in these verses about how children may inherit an unhealthy legacy. That will be a theme that runs throughout the Book of Mormon, a text in which the hatred of Lehi's sons for each other gets passed down for hundreds of years. But the beauty of the story is when we see the inbreaking of God in releasing the children from the sins of their parents. Later in the narrative, we will see periods in which the gospel gives people the strength they need to let go of the bias and hatred and patterns of marginalization that were passed down to them. God sets us free, breaking the generational chains of prejudice that were never ours to carry, even when we unknowingly repeated it. The Nephites may not be ready for it here, but eventually the lines between the groups will be torn down and the people will be bonded together.

Jacob 3:14

The prevalent theme of this chapter is generational legacy: how some of what we inherit is unhealthy and destructive, and what we do with that inheritance and who is held accountable for it. This last verse serves as a perfect metaphor for that theme: Jacob is writing his own words, but the plates that he writes on were made by Nephi. The foundational material he is using was crafted by Nephi, his elder brother and mentor. There is a fundamental ideology that he is carrying over to his own prophetic era. The ideas of Nephi—including his hatred and othering of groups of people—will be handed down, like the plates themselves, through the rest of the Book of Mormon. In some ways, the gifts of our ancestors are good. But we also get a lot of mess built into the good. That's why we believe in continuing revelation and hope that revelation releases us from the past. That's not to say that the prophets of old weren't good people or didn't perform miracles. It's simply to accept that they were human and now we have a responsibility to free ourselves and the next generation from harmful and hateful ideologies. There will be times in the Book of Mormon that we will see that liberation in glorious ways.

Jacob 4:3-4

Jacob's hope that his descendants will be grateful for the work he has done and look at his actions with joy is another example of how the prophetic is a journey in parenting. Jacob likely also realizes that his descendants will feel frustration with his mistakes. But he takes this time to remind us how hard the work is and to pray that we will understand and find joy from his words. While less explicit than Nephi's apology for mistakes,[10] Jacob is adding his plea to readers of this text that they will extend mercy toward him. There's an implied message: there will be things here that you may find contemptible or sorrowful. Try to learn with joy, because this work was extremely hard. Just know that we knew the Savior and that sharing our "hope of his glory" was the intent of our hearts.

Jacob 4:6-10

Prophetic power can nudge the world. How often do prophets need to literally move mountains or turn the waves back on themselves? It may be possible, but it's not common. The everyday work of prophets is to move people into beloved community, to prod them toward repenting and changing their mindsets. This kind of internal work is just as challenging as moving trees. Any kind of social justice work of asking people to let go of cultural constructs and internalized prejudice is pushing back against the basic nature of human behavior. Moving people into repentance and into a life with God is miraculous. Jacob knows this particularly well because of his audience. He realizes that it would take the power of God to shift the Nephite men away from the way they've been thinking about women.

---

10. 1 Nephi 19:6

Verse 7 emphasizes how grace underlines every movement of seas and mountains in our lives. Seeing our weaknesses is a powerful gift that God shares so that we know how to do better. Our power to change ourselves ultimately comes through the grace of God. Our journey with God—even a journey that includes moving mountains, trees, and waves—will not look perfect all the time, but grace gives us strength in our weakness.

There is a word of warning in verse 8 for those who have done this work with God: even after going through this process of seeing your own weakness and moving the mountains inside yourself, don't think that you know all of God's ways or how God will move with everyone. There is a depth to God that is unfathomable. Even those who experience transformational revelation will not get it all. No single person can know all the ways of God, so no one person has the totality of truth. Our charge, then, is to be careful to not despise the revelations of God. That may be the revelations that convict us, the ones intended for our own souls. Or it may be the ones for others, that will look unfamiliar to our own eyes.

Sometimes we wonder how justice and mercy can coexist peacefully. We get a hint in verse 10, where Jacob tells us that God counsels in wisdom, justice and mercy. Wisdom is the third leg of the stool. Justice and mercy don't go together on their own, but with divine wisdom they become a powerful tool.[11]

Jacob 4:11

We should never tire of the phrase "beloved brethren" in scripture. Although the wording excludes women, it's still a beautiful way of offering love to a community. The phrase does not appear at all in the Old Testament and just 11 times in the New Testament, but it appears in the Book of Mormon 74 times. Jacob and Nephi consistently use it, even when their people are acting terribly. It is worth

---

11. For more on this idea, read the section on Jacob 6:10.

noting that these prophets can simultaneously rebuke the people and yet still call them beloved.[12]

Jacob 4:13

Prophets speak truth as it really is. The adversary may make things look muddied or hazy, but the Spirit acts as a cleaner to remove everything that obscures our vision.[13] For those who see God in that work, the Spirit is the wisdom, mentioned in verse 10, that clears our lenses of the world and allows us to see where justice and mercy need to happen.

Jacob 4:14

Jacob notes that the Jews were a stiff-necked people. In this record, we will also see the Nephites and Lamanites act as stiff-necked people. At times each of us is likely stiff-necked. In chapter 3, Jacob condemned the Lamanites for their filthiness before mentioning that his own people were even filthier. He has a tendency to deal in comparative terms of groups of people, which is not always healthy. When we are calling out another community on their failings, it's likely that we fail in the same ways.

"Looking beyond the mark" is sometimes used as a criticism against those who wrestle with scripture or doctrine. The claim is that if God's word is simple, then engaging in struggle and analysis is making things too complicated. The answer of whether seeing complication is problematic lies in the motivation for doing so—whether we are seeing complexity as a way to understand God better or to avoid obedience to simple commandments. Sometimes we have a

---

12. There is a shadow of God's love in that—it echoes Romans 8:39: "Nor height, nor depth, nor any living creature, shall be able to separate us from the love of God." Even when you are far off course, you are still beloved.
13. In social justice terms, we would describe this as being "woke"—seeing more clearly what is happening around you.

tendency to take plain and simple truth and use complicating factors as a reason for not following them.[14]

Jacob 4:15–18

As the framing for the allegory of the olive trees, the last four verses of chapter 4 ought to be included in the beginning of chapter 5. The allegory is an answer to the question of how a group of people who have rejected God may become unified with the Divine. Jacob is going to teach us how God continues to work with all God's children.

Jacob 5

The allegory in Jacob 5 has boundless interpretations. Through a social justice lens, it is a text of comfort: an explanation of how God works with us in our labors and provides hope and respite during difficult times. This reading will see the Lord of the vineyard as God or Christ and the servant as anyone who is trying to make the world more just and merciful. For those who are weary in the work, Jacob 5 can remind us that God struggles, weeps, grieves, and ultimately finds joy. It is a balm for anyone who is unsettled by the state of the world.

Jacob 5:4

Before the servant even arrives, the Lord is at work. The variety of active verbs in this chapter is lovely: prune, dig, nourish, pluck, graft, preserve, labor, gather, plant. The Lord is a caretaker and a laborer before the servant ever begins. This is important for anyone who

---

14. For example, "love thy neighbor" is a plain and simple truth. It ought not to be complicated to put that into practice by saying "we will not allow the state to separate children from their parents at the border." In this case, looking beyond the mark means saying, "But then what do we do about immigration? How can we keep people out if they can simply use children to claim asylum?" Through wickedness, basic decency and humanity become convoluted ideas. In these cases, we complicate wickedness *for the purpose* of excusing it. This is looking beyond the mark because of blindness.

feels alone in the work. God is with you. God has been doing this work from the beginning and will continue on until the end.

Jacob 5:7

Pay attention to the closeness of the relationship between the Lord and the servant throughout the chapter. At times the Lord heeds the servant, other times the servant listens to the Lord. There is a back-and-forth between them about what they should do and then a united effort to carry it out. They both seem to see their work as a partnership.

This is the first time we see the Lord grieve for the fruit of the vineyard, but it will happen many times throughout the chapter. This tells us that it is not unusual for God to grieve. We believe in a God who weeps. Jesus wept during his mortality. And the brother of Jared's vision in Ether includes God weeping for the world. We have to note that the work of God is a work of grief. Righteous work and grief go hand-in-hand: creation followed by grief, long and hard labor followed by grief, reviewing the fruit and grief. That deep sadness will be the prevailing emotion through the allegory—and for good reason, because the Lord and servant work so hard and fail again and again.[15]

Jacob 5:11

The Lord of the vineyard says repeatedly that he would grieve the loss of a tree. It makes no difference if the tree is full of decay and putting out bad fruit and seems to only cause additional work without good results. There is never a moment of not caring whether even the least productive tree lives or dies. This is an amazing example of how we

---

15. Through a social justice lens, Jacob 5 is an exploration of what it is to do God's work on earth. It should be no surprise to us that so many of the prophets speak of being weighed down or troubled. The Lord speaks to his servant of his grief. Trying and failing is the ongoing narrative of working for justice.

can think about people in our work, especially the ones who are the most frustrating or heart-breaking. Not every tree will produce good fruit, but each one is precious to the master.

Jacob 5:15

Notice the plural nature of the Lord's invitation. Let us go down. Let us work. Let us labor. Throughout the allegory, the Lord co-labors alongside the servant, without regard to station or hierarchy. Any kind of righteous work is a co-labor. And if you're in the midst of that, struggling with the burden of how much work there is to be done, there is nothing more beautiful than God saying "we." You are doing it together.

Jacob 5:17

The Lord's pronouncement of good fruit echoes of Genesis, when God reviews God's creations and states that they are good. This is the way God seems to work, with a constant cycle of creation, review, labor, and review. We should follow the same pattern. There must be times in our work when we review what we've done with God and ask if it is good. The allegory tells us that the Lord and servant taste the fruit, check the roots, and examine the branches. They are careful and honest about the results of their work, not just at the end but throughout, checking in again and again along all the stages. It's important to pause sometimes in the work and look at whether what we are doing is good.

Jacob 5:21-22

Now we get the servant questioning the Lord, wondering why he chose such a poor spot for planting. The servant seems to be feeling some frustration with the futility of the work. The Lord responds, "Counsel me not; I knew that it was a poor spot of ground." This is the only time that the Lord rebukes the servant or invokes a greater knowledge of the vineyard. In our own lives, we may look at the darkness of the world and ask, "How could anything thrive in this place? Am I wasting my time?" But from even the poorest and hardest of circumstances, God can make things thrive. We can trust that God knows what is possible.

Jacob 5:26–27

Here the narrative flips and it's the Lord who feels despairing and the servant who offers hope. This exchange is a testament to the power of a working relationship with God, one that offers us the ability to sometimes ask God for more grace in our call. We can ask, "God, can I try this? I want to stay a little longer here, even though it doesn't seem to be working. Can you give me your blessing to keep going?" and God relinquishes something and lets us continue that work. At this point in the allegory, the Lord not only acquiesces, but continues as a co-laborer in the work, trying to save the tree because the servant believes in it.

Jacob 5:31–34

After much more work, the Lord and the servant again review the fruit and find this time that none of it is good. So after all their labor, the results are all bad. The tree has produced an abundance of fruit but all of it is terrible. In our own work, we may put in enormous amounts of energy and resources and not get the results that we want. While this may feel like our own failing, it may be comforting to realize that this happens even to the Lord of the vineyard. Even God may work hard and have things not turn out the right way. We need to know that laboring in the kingdom doesn't guarantee a happy ending. That may be the most sobering message of the allegory.

Then the Lord asks the servant for advice about what to do. As much as God is omniscient, there may also be times in which God moves in questions with us. We can engage in a dialogue about how to move forward on difficult issues. Part of that dialogue may be God asking us: What shall we do?[16]

Jacob 5:41–50

The Lord of the vineyard wept. Again, notice the deep grief inherent in this work. And then notice how God takes all of the responsibility. While the Lord invites the servant to do the work together, when it fails, he reverts to the singular pronoun: "What could *I* have done more for my vineyard?" (emphasis added).

The verses that follow are the Lord's lament. Just as various prophets have, at times, despaired at their failings or inadequacies, the Lord comes to a point of absolute hopelessness with the work. Notice the structure of the lament: first, the Lord faces how hard the work is going to be from the beginning. Second, the Lord lists everything that has done. Then the Lord refers to the witness to testify about everything that he has done. Third, the Lord acknowledges the feelings of sadness. This is the outline for processing the darkest moments of work that will sometimes feel soul-wrenching. These are the words we can use for despair.

At the end of lament, God says for the third time in seven verses, "What more could I have done?" Sometimes we will simply come to the end of the list of ways we can fight for change. And yet here the servant is able to offer a little bit of hope: "Spare it a little longer." Hold on. No new answers or ideas, just keep going.

---

16. The servant is so deeply invested in the work. They are a good steward. The strength of the relationship between the Lord and the servant lies in how much they both care about the vineyard. The way the servant presents ideas to the Lord is reminiscent of the brother of Jared taking stones to the Lord for light. Sometimes we think that all of our inspiration or instruction needs to come from God. But when we're engaged in the dialogue with God, we can take our wild and beautiful ideas to God and say, "I have this problem and here's my idea. Will you touch it and make it divine? Will you co-labor with me so that we can solve this together?" And sometimes the divine response will be, "Alright, I got you. Let's do it."

Jacob 5:70

Finally, near the end, the Lord asks the servant to call in more help. We can call in our people who we know can help us do the work. Sometimes the work will be isolating, but we should know the community we can call on when it's needed. And yet, there may be only a few who show up, even when we call for help, so even this offer of hope is tempered.

Jacob 5:71-72

Given how difficult and long the work has been, the confidence with which the Lord promises joy following the labors seems surprising. Why should they have belief in future good fruit when there's been no evidence of good results in the past? Despite the Lord's lament, hope abides. And yet this hope comes with additional labor. Alongside the newly recruited servants, the Lord works hard right up until the end. For all of the dismal outcomes, the Lord has never left the vineyard. Sometimes the nearest we come to God are in the hardest things we do and with the worst results, because those dark places are where the Lord has been working. And if we continue to work alongside God, we can partake of that hope for future joy.

Jacob 5:75-77

The Lord and the servants reap the joy of good fruit. For awhile. The Lord, looking toward the future, says that he expects to have a period of good harvest, but that it will not last forever. The work never completely ends and conditions do not consistently improve. Evil fruit will return to the vineyard. So there will be good times, times of enjoying the hard-fought victories, but the work will continue. The only constant is that the Lord remains in the vineyard, working alongside us as we work with patience and hope.

Jacob 6

Chapter 6 is essentially a very brief review of the vineyard allegory, followed by Jacob's conclusions. In reading this chapter, it's useful to place Jacob back into the context prior to the allegory: he is speaking to a society that has become deeply entrenched in behaviors that are offensive to God. His prophetic voice here is coming from a place of condemnation of his people. Chapter 6 ought to be read as Jacob applying the vineyard allegory to the Nephite men who need to repent, not as the definitive and singular understanding of Jacob 5.

Jacob 6:4

If we take one thing from the allegory, it should be an understanding of how merciful God is and how God remembers us and works endlessly in the vineyard. For the Lord and the servant, remembering the vineyard did not simply happen once, at the end of time. Remembering happened again and again, with the Lord and servant returning to check on and nurture the trees many times. This tells us that "to remember" means consistent care, an action that encompasses all the labor that needs to be done for an individual or a community. The Book of Mormon repeatedly exhorts its readers to remember.

The imagery in the rest of this verse is beautifully evocative, as it uses the human body to describe the way God reaches out to us. The final clause exemplifies God's inclusive love. Anyone who does not harden their hearts shall be saved.

Jacob 6:5-6

Jacob often uses language of the heart as a metaphor for our relationship with God. Here, he calls on his people to not only soften their hearts, but to "come [to God] with full purpose of heart,"—to entirely commit themselves to the Divine. But even when we cleave unto God, a verb that evokes an urgency and a binding, we are only beginning to love God as much as God loves us. Even in this community's sin and brokenness, Jacob lets these people know how much they are loved.[17]

Jacob 6:9–10

Notice that it's "the power of the redemption and the resurrection" that will bring shame to some people. This is the shame that comes in knowing what God has done on our behalf and also knowing that we haven't taken what has been offered. The shame comes from inside ourselves: a regret for our misuse of a divine gift.

Jacob 6:10

Jacob speaks a great deal about mercy and about God reaching out to us all the day long. But here he states very clearly the necessity for justice. There is a power to justice and it "cannot be denied." If you bring forth evil fruit, no matter how much God has labored, how many times God has invited you to feast at God's table, how tirelessly God's servant has worked for you, there will come a time in which God can't deny justice. This may be hard to hear—we tend to prefer words of mercy and forgiveness. Yet there is an important way in which justice and mercy are tied together.

Consider the Nephite women and children who are present at Jacob's sermon. Those who have been abused, wronged, or marginalized in some way may understand justice very differently from those who have enacted that harm. For those who have been suffering for a long time, watching their abusers escape any form of justice may feel very wrong. Feeling as if righteousness must be equated only with forgiveness and mercy is a heavy burden to bear, particularly for those on the margins. Victims may go their entire lives seeing the structures

---

17. Jacob's heart question in verse 6 sounds like people who suffer from atherosclerosis, a hardening of their arteries from the slow buildup of fat deposits. Those with physically or spiritually constricted hearts cannot receive the nutrients they need to live. Jacob is asking his community to take serious action to repair their hearts in order to survive.

of power meant to protect them instead offer their aggressors no redress. Knowing that even God cannot deny justice can be a comfort for those who have been deeply oppressed and violated. They may not see justice during their lifetimes, but eventually, the voices from the dust will cry out against those who have caused harm. This makes justice a form of mercy. Justice and mercy are not oppositional: they are inseparably connected in the way God moves with us.

Jacob 6:12-13

Jacob's final question rings of the Lord of the vineyard, asking what more he could have done. Jacob cannot say any more to his people—and to us—than to be wise. Being wise is a commandment! Interestingly, the injunction is not to be obedient. Jacob has laid out various choices and the consequences that attend them. Now, he asks for the people to be wise in what they choose. The final sentence of his sermon is one last reminder: the bar of God may be pleasing or dreadful, depending on what we do with our hearts.

Jacob 7:3-4

Carefully examine any theology that strokes your ego or tells you all is well or doesn't challenge you in hard ways to see how you can do better by God and fellow humans. In the beginning of Jacob we read about how the corruption of the Nephite society began with pride. Sherem seems attuned to this, understanding that these people are easily led to lifting themselves up and creating social hierarchies. Sherem is hard-working, learned, and charming and he is using flattery to lead the people astray. Pride is consistently a threat to any faith journey.

Jacob 7:6-8

Notice that Sherem calls Jacob "Brother Jacob." This is a term of familiarity, the language of the church and of common cause. Jacob must have had good reason for devoting a portion of the limited space on the plates to Sherem's words. Jacob finds these words important for us to read. We can assume that the reason is that Sherem is a template for one way in which people are lured away from doing the work of God. We can read his words as a warning for what we may see in our own faith communities. First, Sherem uses flattery, both with the people in general and with Jacob in particular. Second, Sherem attempts to turn good evil and evil good. He tells Jacob that the work Jacob has been doing in calling people to repentance is actually perversion. Third, Sherem quotes scripture, warping the words of God to shame Jacob. Finally, and most importantly, Sherem's argument rests in using the law to deny the power of Christ.[18]

Jacob 7:13-14

This is a particularly stinging taunt for Jacob, who is a scriptorian and seems to value knowledge so much. Sherem's words are reminiscent of three temptations of Christ.[19] Asking for a sign from God is such a dangerous and easy temptation because it is, fundamentally, about abandoning faith. It is about requiring proof of what you already know about your relationship with God.

Jacob knows that Sherem knows God. Jacob's indictment of Sherem is not that Sherem doesn't understand God, but that Sherem is denying the divine truths he has already learned. What truths do we know about God that we are willing to abandon in the face of being offered an easier story?

---

18. Beware those who would place laws and rules above the gospel and would attempt to flatter away or shame those who testify of Christ. There are people who will use the things of God against the people of God. To weaponize scripture by denying someone's spiritual experiences or to place the law above the gospel is spiritual abuse. The example of Sherem should make us wary of anyone who uses theological underpinnings to proclaim an anti-Christ theology. We need to be careful of anyone who teaches a doctrine that rests on flattering its followers and embracing the law over the message of Christ's teachings.
19. Matthew 4

Jacob 7:17-23

Sherem reveals a little of his past here: he has previously witnessed the power of the Holy Ghost and experienced the ministering of angels. This is someone who was close to God and likely knew Jacob well. His deathbed confession reveals more of his importance to the community. His willingness to acknowledge the harm he has caused his community and attempt to make it right through an apology has enormous influence on the people. Far from a collective shrug at Sherem's words and death, the Nephites are so overcome that they restore "peace and the love of God," something that Jacob has been working toward for a long time. The fact that Sherem was able to use his last words to reestablish peace, love, and faith undermines Jacob's claim that Sherem was a "wicked man." He may have had a wicked season and done terrible things, but in his last moments, God was there.

Jacob 7:24-25

Here we have Nephite evangelism for the first time. Not only was it unsuccessful, it appears actually to have precipitated additional violence. We know from Jacob's words that the Nephites hate the Lamanites and believe that the Lamanites are filthy and cursed. Such beliefs are not conducive to sharing the gospel message. The Nephites have experienced a change of heart and have begun the repentance process within their own community. But they have not accepted the movement of the gospel that would do the work of uprooting their deep prejudice and discrimination. That internal work needs to happen before anyone sets out to do missionary work. When it doesn't, and evangelism happens in a backwards way, don't expect a lot of success. It's not at all surprising that the Nephites' missionary efforts here failed. How you bring the gospel matters, and the Nephites haven't addressed the hate they carry in their hearts.[20]

---

20. Compare this experience to when the sons of Mosiah go to the Lamanites, ready to serve and love them. In that instance, there is a powerful inbreaking of the gospel

Jacob 7:26–27

As is common for the Book of Mormon prophets, Jacob offers his own apology for the potential failures of his record when he states, "I have written according to the best of my knowledge." He knows he may have been wrong in some ways, but he did the best he could with what he had.

The rest of his words are the beautiful farewell of a man who felt like a wanderer all of his life. He was born in tribulation, during the saddest time of his father's life, and "suffered afflictions and much sorrow" in childhood.[21] These are the words of a refugee, a man whose life was marked with wilderness, abuse, death, separation of family, and the misdeeds of his people. When he writes that "our lives passed away like as it were unto us a dream, we being a lonesome and solemn people, wanderers, cast out from Jerusalem, born in tribulation, in a wilderness, and hated of our brethren . . . wherefore, we did mourn out our days," we can hear the deep grief that undergirds his life. He has never felt settled. Even as he seeks God, and as the Nephites find a place where they can be safe, Jacob feels like he has mourned out his days. Jacob's life has been deeply hard. We might expect that someone who has studied scripture so carefully and worked so hard to know God would somehow escape suffering. Jacob's life tells us otherwise. He never seems to settle into a place called home.[22]

---

and many people are converted. It's possible that during Jacob's time the Lamanites simply weren't ready to listen, but it's also possible that they are sensing that at this time, there's not actually a lot of good will or self-reflection from the Nephite people. One of the hints that we get that it may be the latter is that Jacob describes the end result of this bout of violence as the Nephites being "conquerors of their enemies." Not only does this attempt at missionary work provoke violence, but the Nephites respond by conquering, rather than loving, their enemies.

21. 2 Nephi 2:1

22. We know that people who don't feel a sense of safety and belonging as children struggle to feel those things as adults. Jacob was born in the wilderness and he effectively remains in that wilderness all of his life.

ENOS

Enos 1:1

As Nephi did, Enos includes reference to his parents and what they did for him as he introduces himself. It's striking that although Jacob had a life burdened by violence, instability, and grief, he passed on goodness to his child. Enos even blesses God in gratitude for his father.[1] In the midst of a life of harrowing experiences, Jacob raised a child who felt nurtured with God. That's a powerful thing for a child to say.

Enos 1:2–3

Enos tells us directly that he is going to describe his own wrestle with God. His narrative is a transparent description of his spiritual journey and he gives us the behind-the-scenes account, not one that looks finished and flawless. Enos is not the first writer to use the verb "wrestle" (think of Jacob wrestling the angel in the Old Testament) to describe his experiences with the Divine, and we should take the word seriously. A journey with God is often grueling and painful and you don't walk away the same person.

---

1. It would have been a valuable contribution if, as Nephi did, Enos also referenced his mother as well.

Note that Enos was hunting beasts at the time that he was prompted to pray and then received great inspiration. Despite Nephi's earlier statement about hunting being a sign of Lamanite filthiness,[2] it appears that the Nephites also hunt. While Nephi objects specifically to the Lamanites hunting "beasts of prey,"[3] any perceived difference between types of animals would stem from cultural mores, not a strong divine preference. This is a detail that tells us that at least some of the Book of Mormon's criticisms of the Lamanites are from human cognitive dissonance and prejudice, not from God. This relationship is more complex than the text initially leads readers to believe. We elaborate on this concept further in verses 20–23.

In addition to what Enos has already said about his father, here we read that Jacob spoke of "the joy of the saints." Contrast this to Jacob's final words, in which he described the Nephites as "a lonesome and a solemn people."[4] The lonely, wandering prophet spoke not only of grief, but also of radical joy. And it's the words of joy that prick Enos's heart and prompt him to listen to the Spirit. To underline Jacob's role in this moment, Enos writes that Jacob's words "sunk deep into my heart." Jacob frequently used the heart as a metaphor for spiritual work.[5] This father-son relationship is beautifully outlined in just a few verses.

Enos 1:4

Nephi, Jacob, and now Enos have all described crying in some way. In Enos' case, this sounds like more of an emotional call than a weeping, but both are a vulnerable moment of raising one's voice to the heavens. That kind of intense emotion, the breaking down of the facade of being entirely capable and in control, provides a lovely example to us of the humanity of these prophets. They reach out to God in

---

2. Such as in 2 Nephi 5:21–25
3. 2 Nephi 5:24
4. Jacob 7:26
5. See, for example, Jacob 6

desperation because they don't know how to handle the struggles of their lives. They don't always have the answers or know where to turn. Even in this moment, Enos prays for a period with the feeling that his cries are not breaking the atmosphere, that perhaps there's a sense of physical distance that even prayer cannot bridge. It is only when night comes, after a day of intense work, that Enos feels that his voice rises up and reaches God.[6]

Enos 1:7

Enos' conversation with God here echoes the conversation that Mary will have with the angel Gabriel: upon hearing of a miraculous change upon them, their first reaction is, "But how did that happen?" In neither case does God resent or reject the question.

Enos 1:8–13

Scripture repeatedly differentiates between being healed and being whole. We see it in the story of the ten lepers,[7] in which ten men are healed from their illness but only one, the one who returns with gratitude, is pronounced "whole." Jesus' miracle heals all of the men, but it is the faith of the one that makes wholeness. Here, Enos is also healed miraculously (this time from the sickness of sin), but God pronounces Enos "whole" as a function of his faith. Healing is the first step toward wholeness, but faith is required for it to be complete. This makes us a partner with God in the process of becoming whole. We may be passive recipients of the grace of healing, but wholeness requires an exertion of our own faith and gratitude.

As soon as Enos receives this great gift, he wants it for his brethren. After his first burst of curiosity about how it happened, his immedi-

---

6. We may experience that kind of hopelessness in our own lives and notice that our own prayers do not always feel fully embodied. That's okay. It happens to our prophets.
7. Luke 17:11–19

ate reaction is to ask, "How can this miracle spread? How can others experience what I have experienced?" This is the rooting of good evangelism, based on a person's gratitude for the gifts of God and a love for other people. Enos starts with his own people, understanding that the Nephites have apparently not experienced true conversion, that they are not yet whole.

In verse 4, Enos' soul was hungry and seeking. In verse 9, Enos has been made whole, and he immediately "pour[s] out [his] whole soul unto God" for his brethren. He takes the wholeness he has received and shares it. Healing begets healing and wholeness begets wholeness. Enos' vocabulary around his soul has changed during his dialogue with the Divine. When we pray for one another, we ought to do it as whole souls, because we have consistently sought forgiveness and subsequently felt God sweeping away our guilt and endowing us with a desire to give our whole souls to others.

Enos' heart is expanding in this process, as evidenced by his thoughts turning gradually further outward. He describes the Lamanites as his brethren, even though they are currently in a deeply adversarial relationship. Enos went to the woods to talk to God about himself, but the longer he talks with the Divine, the more he thinks about others.

Verse 12 shows us just how much Enos and his faith have grown. But it is verse 13 that is theologically stunning. In verse 12, the Lord offers Enos the desires of his heart. Out of everything that Enos could ask for, he asks that if the Nephites are destroyed, that their records will be preserved as a testament for the Lamanites. Enos' view is so long and his heart so compassionate that his greatest desire if for his enemies to receive help from the work of his people. This should give each of us pause. Those of us engaged in social justice work do not usually think about whether we would be willing, if we failed, to hand over the work of our lives to be of benefit to the forces against which we struggle. It's a powerful thing to think that the record of your people would help your enemies come to God. This tells what kind of human Enos is, and particularly what a "whole" soul looks like. This is the desire of a whole soul. This is the kind of love we seek after.

Enos 1:16–18

There are two theologically fascinating pieces of this verse. First, Enos created the terms of a covenant that was the desire of his heart, and God agreed to it. This is extraordinary—covenants do not usually include human input. With such a short record of Enos, we can only speculate on what was so special about him that he had the privilege of doing this kind of work with God.

Second, God promises to protect this record *as part of a covenant with Enos and Enos' ancestors*. Does this mean that all the Book of Mormon writers that followed took part in this covenant, similar to the descendants of Abraham, who live under the Abrahamic covenant? Does that also bring anyone who reads the Book of Mormon as scripture under that same covenant? It seems that this record exists because of the covenants of Enos and his ancestors. By reading this book as holy text, are we not all moving in the covenant of Enos? The theological richness of this text, the increased understanding it gives of the way God interacts with humans, should give us pause.

Enos is able to rest once he knows that the Nephites' record will be preserved. Even though his people may be destroyed at the hands of the Lamanites, Enos' soul rests. This covenant does not protect Enos from a life of warring with the Lamanites. The Nephites will not survive. But their record will be used well, so Enos can rest. Covenants with God will not eliminate the struggles in our lives and the sacrifices that we will have to make. But Enos teaches us that what can give our souls rest is that all will be well in the end.[8]

---

8. For those of us in the struggle for justice, we may have to simply believe God that all will be well, even if it's not in our lifetimes, and even if our work is not used in the way that we would hope for at first. Enos' words sound similar to those of Martin Luther King's last sermon, in which he said that black Americans would reach "the

Enos 1:20-23

The number of direct parallels between negative descriptions of the Lamanites and the record we have of Lehi's family in the wilderness is striking. Enos writes that the Lamanites dwell in tents, wander in the wilderness, have skill with a hunting bow, and eat raw meat. These are all things specifically mentioned in Nephi's narrative about his family. We cannot know if this was done consciously or unconsciously on Enos' part, but it is striking that these qualities were considered neutral descriptions when Lehi's family did them, but are signs of degeneracy when the Lamanites do them. Again, this looks more like the writer's bias against people he has been taught to demean and less like a legitimate critique. Enos also invokes the Lamanites' clothing and hair as a signal of their immorality. To modern ears, this will sound merely like ethnocentrism, evidence that Enos, mired in cultural prejudice, could not see the Lamanites clearly.

While in verse 21 Enos describes the Nephites as some kind of idyllic agrarian society, verses 22 and 23 complicate that narrative, letting us know that the Nephites had problems of their own. The Nephite prophets sound frustrated with the people, offering harsh rebukes about death and eternity at every turn. Here is yet another example of a Nephite prophet first condemning the Lamanites, then admitting to the poor condition of the Nephites. And yet none of the Nephites' unrighteousness is attributed to raising goats or wearing loin cloths.

The authors of the Book of Mormon do not see their own prejudice and how it allows them to link sin, which is universal, to specific cultural practices, which are particular. Once again, we see the humanness of the prophets of the Book of Mormon and how the Divine mixes fluidly with frailty. Enos may have had extraordinary faith and a deep relationship with God, but he still inherited bad

---

promised land," although he did not know if he would live long enough to see it. This is what Enos is saying—that he can rest because good will happen eventually.

ideas and made mistakes of his own. Our work is to separate out what will lead us closer to God and what to set aside.

Enos 1:27

While the words are somewhat different, the closing ideas of Enos' book sound similar to those of Jacob and Nephi: he is looking for rest. These are the words of someone who has lived a life full of hardship and war. His desire is for peace. Those who have struggled during mortality seem particularly inclined to see eternity as a chance for rest and comfort. We may trust that it shall be so for them.

JAROM

Jarom 1:2

Possibly due to Enos' covenant with God, the language about the purpose of this record has changed. Jarom is the first writer to state that "these things are written for the intent of the benefit of our brethren the Lamanites." So there's a shift in the language about why this record exists. That change in intent is going to affect how the authors approach their work.

Jarom 1:3-5

The writers of the Book of Mormon frequently try to describe the level of righteousness of an entire people. These verses are a good example of how difficult that is: in verse 3, the people sound desperately wicked. In verse 4, there are many who are receiving spiritual guidance and revelations. In verse 5, the people are obeying a strict law of Moses. So the standard of righteousness may be difficult to define, but there's the added problem of the complexity of each individual and the diversity of a large number of people. It's probably fair to say that any attempt at describing the righteousness of an entire society is going to be absurdly reductive. That's a useful point to remember throughout this text.

Jarom 1:8–9

These are two verses of the Book of Mormon that need to be closely examined because this is the first time that wealth, violence, and God are tied so closely together. First, the Nephites are closely linking exceeding wealth to weaponizing a community. As they grow rich, they seem to automatically increase their armaments. This in itself should make us wary. Second, to have victory in war attributed to God being on your side is deeply problematic. The logical conclusion is that anyone winning in war must be righteous—that military success is, in itself, a sign of God's favor. That's a corrupt theology and one that the writers of the Book of Mormon repeatedly espouse. It attaches God to violence and power in unhealthy ways. A brief examination of world history quickly reveals that righteousness and victory in violence are not necessarily correlated.

A closer examination of the context of these verses underscores how, on a practical level, this theology is dangerous. In verse 3, Jarom makes clear that the Nephites are not a particularly righteous society. Yet just a few verses later, their wealth and their success in war is given as evidence that they *are* virtuous. They see themselves as righteous not because they are actually seeking after God or living Christlike lives, but because they have wealth and military success. That is fundamentally the problem with using those things as markers of God's favor: it allows the bad to call itself good. It's human to take worldly concepts of success and attach God's name to it, but it's forcing God into a space where God does not belong.

The writers of the Book of Mormon will repeatedly use the phrase "prosper in the land" to describe winning wars and gaining extreme wealth. This misunderstanding of what it means to prosper in the land has ripple effects down the generations. Jarom isn't speaking here about prospering in the land as having enough food to care for the poor or caring for the land so that it is healthy and abundant. Having that kind of definition of prospering in the land would fundamentally change the goals of the Nephite society. They would see

God's promises to the righteous as being about creating a beloved, sustainable community. This would prompt a change in their priorities, shifting from having "precious things" and "weapons of war" to managing the land and their society so that everyone is safe and valued. They would create the kind of society that eventually happens in 4 Nephi, when Jesus shows them a better understanding of prospering in the land.

OMNI

Omni 1:1-2

Each writer in the Book of Mormon introduces the book describing a slightly different purpose. Jarom has written that it is a record for the Lamanites; Omni writes that it is to preserve his people's genealogy. Later in this book, Chemish will write that he is keeping a record simply because that's what his fathers told him to do. It's worth recognizing that not all scriptural texts were written with the same goal in mind. It helps us remember that each writer has different priorities, meaning that each writer will filter his work differently. As readers, we can be grateful when the authors name their purpose for writing because it helps us understand the text. In Omni, none of the writers claim the mantle of the prophetic in the ways that Nephi, Jacob, and Enos did. They do not describe their conversations and covenants with God, nor do they call the people to repentance. This appears to simply be a passing off of the plates from father to son. It's a record of a people, not a prophetic journey. So it's understandable that there are shifts in the tone of the writing as there are shifts in the purpose of the plates.

At the same time, there's something beautiful in the fact that these verses are not omitted from the record, even though these men are not claiming great spiritual heights. In verse 2, Omni admits that he is "a wicked man" and that he has not obeyed God's commandments. This record tells us that it is not only the righteous who get to write scripture! Holy text does not need to be exclusive to spiritual giants. In this moment, we have a wicked man who is admirably honest about his own failings, but is following the request of his father. There's a beautiful expansiveness to that.

Omni 1:5-7

Most of the Book of Omni happens during long stretches of war, occasionally interrupted by ceasefires. The authors of this book are writing through the lens of being soldiers and witnesses to war. Amaron interprets the violence here as destroying the wicked and sparing the righteous. Of course, war does not usually seem to operate in such a surgically precise manner. We know from current events and world history that there are always innocent people who die in war. How can Amaron know, as he claims in verses 5 and 7, who is wicked and who is righteous? Can he see into the heart of every person who has died? That's a ridiculous idea, but it is the logical extension of the idea that God takes sides in war.[1] Amaron is giving us a disturbing insight into how he, and possibly the Nephites, view violence: that it operates as a tool for God to sort out who is good and who is evil.

Amaron repeats the idea of prospering in the land, once again linking this phrase to warfare, just as Jarom did. As we wrote in the section on Jarom, we believe that this idea of "prospering in the land" is misunderstood. But we see here how a poor interpretation of an idea can be passed down from generation to generation and used in wrong ways, in this case to justify violence as God's will. In all their references to "prosper in the land," Lehi and Nephi either didn't define "prosper" or they described it as being kept safe.[2] For Lehi and Nephi, men who spent long stretches of their lives as refugees and victims of abuse, a land of safety would sound like a dream.

---

1. Jarom 1:9
2. 2 Nephi 1:9

For Jarom and Amaron, who are living through generations of bloodshed, it would be very tempting to create a narrative that would make sense of the chaos inherent in war. So in the transfer of authors and change in circumstances, "prospering in the land" morphs from a place of safety to God leading the victors of battle, leaving deeply problematic theology in its wake. As readers, we can stand witness to that, offer a charitable heart to these men who lived in horrific times of violence, and simultaneously push back against the theology that does harm.

Omni 1:12, 15

God has a way, in the Book of Mormon, of moving people out of their homelands and into the wilderness. Although they have established themselves in lands that they believed to be promised to them by God, the Nephites are now forced to flee that space and once again search for safety. They meet the people of Zarahemla, who also had to leave their homeland and come to a new place. This happens frequently enough that we can read it as one of the archetypes of this book. Unchallenged continuity does not seem to be one of the promises of God. We will, at times, have to leave the spaces which we believed were ours and which we believed were permanent, and wander in the wilderness for a time before finding a new home. God has been leading people out of their homelands for a long time.

Omni 1:17–24

Nephi was not eager for his descendants to connect themselves to their Jewish ancestry. And the people of Zarahemla have established a new language, new religion, and customs. Yet this connection is deeply meaningful to them. They have, in a sense, met their own people. That shared far-back history leads them to eventually grow into a single group identity. The first thing they do together is share the stories of their people. For both groups, their history is deeply important. Yet crucially, the history of the people of Zarahemla is edited out of this record. We know that Zarahemla gave an oral history. The stated account of Coriantumr will later be included in the Book of Ether. But the people of Zarahemla are left out and their geneology is forgotten.

We need to remember that this record is an abridgement, and there are inherent judgments about who is included in this holy text. Entire groups of people are essentially erased, moved into the label of "Nephites" for the sake of simplicity, with their experiences and backgrounds hidden from history—notice that in verse 24, there is no longer a reference to the people of Zarahemla. They are reduced to being part of the binary Nephites/Lamanites. This record does not represent everyone, and that's important to notice for any narrative.

In addition to losing their records, the people of Zarahemla appear to lose everything else from their culture. Although they are the original people of that land, the Nephites' king becomes the king of all the people. The Nephites declare Zarahemla's language "corrupted" and "cause that [the people of Zarahemla] should be taught" the Nephites' language. The people of Zarahemla lose their government, faith, language, records, and probably other aspects of their culture. This is an act of colonization, even if the Nephites acted with good intentions.

Omni 1:25–26

This is the first time that inheritance of the plates moves out of a familial pattern. Up to this point, they have been passed to brothers or sons, creating a lineage based on birth rather than merit. For the first time, and possibly because Amaleki has no other choice, the plates go one who is willing to do the work. The plates are breaking from blood lines.

Amaleki is also the first person in a long line of writers who leaves a testimony. He also appears to be familiar with the records, invoking one of the favorite phrases of Jacob ("beloved brethren) and one of Enos' ("whole soul"). Amaleki knows the language of the people who went before him and he is the first writer in a while who seems to understand the spiritual nature of this record and be invested in it. It is perhaps unsurprising that he makes the wise choice of handing off the records to Benjamin.

Omni 1:27–30

This fascinating story is dropped in at the end of this record and is easily overlooked. Yet there is rich meaning here, particularly if we read it with the understanding that this story of people being called out of their homelands and into the wilderness is an archetype of the way God calls us into new spaces. Sometimes God calls us out of places where we are comfortable and that will mean giving up things that we think we ought to possess. Some of the Nephites wanted to go back, wanted to keep hold of what they saw as too valuable to lose. However, they weren't meant to go back. Even though it was their inheritance, something that they believed they were entitled to, God didn't intend for them to possess it.

WORDS OF MORMON

Words of Mormon 1:5–7

Mormon's explanation that he "cannot write the hundredth part of the things" of the Nephites is critically important for understanding scripture. As we read, we need to understand that we are only getting a small fraction of the entirety of what happened to these people. The history of the people and their journeys with God is immense, and a huge percentage is lost. We have to know that any scriptural text is a small sliver of the total, and as such it is coming from a certain angle, usually a singular perspective of the events that happened. We should keep in mind that there were other voices there and other things happening; there are other ways to look at this narrative and other interpretations of its meaning. Therefore, we can understand that this work gives us only a slight glimpse into these people's work with God.

Mormon reinforces this idea by underlining that he has played an active role in choosing what records are most important. We have to know that this record is not only limited to the perspective of the writer, but also filtered through the lens of Mormon. To some extent, we have to trust that Mormon was led by the Spirit to choose wisely. But it is also self-evident that he privileged some voices—particularly the voices of men—over others. What Mormon decided was important to him may leave out words that would have been important to people today. We can still acknowledge that these words were included because Mormon felt them move God into his life. We can appreciate the work Mormon did while also holding space for those voices who were left out.

Words of Mormon 1:8

Mormon's invocation of the word "delightsome" here feels deliberate, as it is a word for describing people in scripture that is particular to Nephi. For Nephi, being delightsome invariably came with being "fair" or "white." Mormon seems to be deliberately separating those words, making it clear that being delightsome, unlike being white or fair, is a temporary status, conditional on one's behavior. The Nephites can be restored to the condition of being delightsome, but skin color is unalterable. This shifting toward a disconnect of those two words matters, because it subtly gives the message that a people can be white and not delightsome, or black and delightsome. Despite how Nephi tied those words together, they are not actually related.[1]

Words of Mormon 1:11

Mormon's phrasing here points to his own continuing prejudice: rather than saying "my people and *our* brethren," he writes, "my people and *their* brethren." The vocabulary tells us that Mormon has lived a life that causes him to want or need to separate himself, even by one degree, from the Lamanites. He is pulling himself out of relationship with them through that wording.

---

1. It is possible that Mormon's ability to deliberately separate these concepts is part of the legacy of Alma, Helaman, and 3 Nephi. Nephi's descendants will do some important work in unpacking Nephi's prejudice and the time of unity among the people following Christ's appearance will alleviate some of that hatred. Mormon is therefore the beneficiary of the healing work of his ancestors.

Words of Mormon 1:13-14

We already knew that the sword of Laban had traveled with Nephi and become an important part of Nephite society as a template for additional weapons.[2] Here, the sword makes an appearance again, this time to lead the Nephites in killing thousands of people. The sword follows this people, a material symbol of the culture of violence that began in their origin story. The sword never becomes Nephi's sword—the ownership is always given back to Laban, a reminder to the people that they were under threat from the beginning and that their patriarch, Nephi, was willing to use murder to protect them and their heritage. The sword always accompanies the plates as a holy object. It is an inheritance of bloodshed.

Notice also that Mormon claims the land of Zarahemla as belonging to the Nephites, despite their having just arrived there from the land that God had promised them. The Nephites lost their land of inheritance as they ran from the Lamanites at the end of Omni. Yet for the rest of the Book of Mormon, Zarahemla will be considered the land of the Nephites. Rather than face the apparent reality that God let them lose their promised land, they simply adopt a new land of inheritance. They have adjusted reality to conform to their narrative.

---

2. 2 Nephi 5:14

CONCLUSION

In 2 Nephi 2:6, Jacob writes that "the Messiah is full of grace and truth." We noted in this book that grace and truth ought to be partners—truth-telling without grace is cruel, while grace without truth is cheap and meaningless. We hope that this text encourages readers to offer grace and truth together, both in scripture study and in life. Hearing and internalizing truth may sometimes be painful—self-awareness of our faults is never comfortable. But God also offers us grace—the binding up and healing of those flaws. Truth does not exist so that we can cast out those who fall short; it exists so that we can all try to do better the next day. The Book of Mormon is an extraordinary example to us of how seeing and naming flaws and still offering grace allows us to learn and grow. None of us measure up to its calls to follow God more closely. Grace is the unearned gift that lets us continue to try.

The first third of the Book of Mormon centers on the origin story of the descendants of Sariah and Lehi. It is a story of wanderers, people who fled violence, journeyed in the wilderness, and sought refuge in a new land. It is a story of a family struggling, and ultimately failing, to stay together. The people we learn about in it, including the prophets, are not perfect. They make mistakes and they suffer. God walks with them anyway.

The Nephites had this record of their origin story. But as we will see in the coming Book of Mormon stories, they didn't internalize it.

They adopted a narrative of prosperity gospel and embraced tribalism. Systemic and overt violence followed. It was not until the appearance of the Savior that, for a time, they managed to heal their divisions and let go of pride.

For those who accept the Book of Mormon as scripture, the book is also part of our origin story. It has been with us since our beginning. The stories provide the foundation for our doctrine, culture, and music. It is a holy text that offers rich meaning to those who are willing to wrestle with it. However, without naming the damaging messages it holds, our people cannot heal from them. Exegeting the Book of Mormon through a lens of social justice provides a salvific message that binds up the wounds of our faith community. The wisdom and strength of the Book of Mormon is an abundant feast, ready and waiting for us to partake.

MARGARET OLSEN HEMMING is the editor in chief of *Exponent II* and sits on the board of the Center for Latter-day Saint Art. She earned a Master's degree in International Peace and Conflict Resolution from American University. She lives in North Carolina with her spouse, three children, and a large vegetable garden.

Made in the USA
Middletown, DE
19 May 2022